Travels in the Loire Valley

The château at Amboise

Travels
in the
Loire Valley

Geoffrey Barlow

Illustrated by Naomi Barlow

MEREHURST PRESS
LONDON

This book is dedicated to Madame Monique Deneux of Paris and Sancerre and Karol Klimek, who first introduced me to the beauty of the Loire valley and also the very wonderful people of the town of Sancerre.

Published 1989 by Merehurst Press
Ferry House, 51-57 Lacy Road
Putney, London SW15 1PR

Co-published in Australia and New Zealand by
Child and Associates
5 Skyline Place, French's Forest
Sydney 2086
Australia

Copyright © Geoffrey Barlow 1989

ISBN 1 85391 036 8

Designed and produced by Snap! Books
Typeset by Maggie Spooner Typesetting
Illustrations by Naomi Barlow
Cover illustration by Charles Claude Pyne (1802–78)
Location: Victoria & Albert Museum/The Bridgeman Art
Library, London
Maps by Sue Lawes
Printed in Great Britain by Butler and Tanner Ltd, Frome

Contents

Acknowledgements

I would like to give my grateful thanks to the following who have helped me in researching this book, and for all their kindness and co-operation.

Hubert Tissier de Mallerais, Director, Comité Du Tourisme et Loisirs Centre Val De Loire; all the tourist offices in the major towns; Theo Kazamias, Hôtel Diderot, Chinon; John-Michel Forest and the Chef, Alain Brisacier, and the Maître d'Hôtel, Daniel Franchineau, of the Hôtel Du Grand Monarque, Azay-le-Rideau; Brittany Ferries; Sealink Dieppe Ferries; the Automobile Association, Newhaven; Air France; the French Tourist Office, London; the staff of East Sussex Libraries; Christiane Bigot, Amboise; Jean Yves; Marec and Catherine Pernet and the Chef, Jean Christophe Beaujeon, at the Auberge La Maison d'Helene, La Verrerie; Count and Countess de Vogué, Château La Verrerie; Joseph Balland, Wine Producer, Bué; Serge Montagu, Wine Producer, St. Gemme; Charlie and Claudine at the Café des Sports, Sancerre; all the management and staff at the hotels and restaurants we visited; Mrs Ann Langley for checking historical facts and Miss Joyce Tobyn for translating the recipes; Mr. Mel Humphrey for checking the Glossary of Motoring Terms; Felicity Clarke and Kim Worts of Snap! Books; Mr and Mrs Malcolm Muggeridge for their encouragement and most of all my wife for not only illustrating this book, but navigating, acting as my secretary, and for reading the proofs.

Geoffrey Barlow

Author's Preface

Like life, holidays are what you make them. Maybe your lifestyle would benefit most from long lazy days sunning on a beach, or perhaps you need the challenge of energetic walks in the mountains. For those of you who are drawn to the Loire valley, you will find a multitude of interests. The river itself must be one of the most beautiful in the world. This royal river with its sandy banks lies at the heart of France.

My family and I have spent many holidays in and around Sancerre. Like most men, I am always in a hurry to reach our destination, despite my wife's protests, as she wants to explore every point of interest on the way. My one thought is to settle in our Gites and unwind.

The return journey is a different matter. Each year we have wandered homeward, making many detours, along the whole of the Loire valley.

In this relaxed state of mind, my wife is able to satisfy her insatiable curiosity about the history of the region, and I have been caught up in her enthusiasm. She likes to find a quiet spot to stop and sketch, while I explore places off the beaten track. We both enjoy sampling the local dishes and of course the wines.

Researching this book has been a great joy. We have travelled our familiar route again, but with much greater awareness. The problem has been what to leave out. It is tempting to overcrowd each day, there is so much to see and do, but you will want to have time to languish by the river and drink in its charm, to wander round quiet flower-decked villages and marvel at the colourful street markets.

Like many of our readers, our command of the French language is limited, but with good will on both sides plus a sense of humour, we manage to communicate, and our efforts are appreciated. So take your phrase book and 'Parlez Français'.

There must be more books written about the valley of the Loire, than any other area of France. Its beauty, climate and accessibility attracted the Kings of France to build their splendid châteaux all along this great river. I have of course included historical notes to whet your appetite. I encountered a few difficulties with translating names and decided to use mainly the French spelling, with the exception of Joan of Arc where I have kept to the familiar English version. For quick reference, I have included a chronology of the French Kings and of the well-known events in the life of Joan of Arc. I have included a bibliography, as I am sure that your curiosity will be aroused and you will want to read in depth about the history of all the châteaux you will be visiting. As there are so many, it has been difficult to decide which ones to pass by. This twelve-day tour is proposed as a holiday and holidays are not enjoyable if the balance is wrong. To prevent you returning home exhausted, and to ensure variety, I suggest that some châteaux you view as you pass by, some you visit the gardens only, and at others you see everything.

The tour begins in Angers and follows the Loire (and some of its tributaries) westwards to Sancerre in 12 days. A postscript takes you to end the tour at Bourges, where you are well placed for returning north to Paris and UK. Throughout the text we have recommended hotels and restaurants: we have awarded each our private star rating based on our feelings of comfort, luxury and value for money.

I hope this book will convey why I love the Loire valley so much, and that you will come to share my feeling and will return many, many times in the future. Who knows, you may possibly meet me in Sancerre, if so, please introduce yourself, as you now know all my favourite haunts. I wish you a very happy and enjoyable holiday, and I must also include the same sentiments from my wife who produced all the drawings for this book.

Vive la Val de Loire, Vive la France.

Geoffrey Barlow
Sancerre, France

Introduction to the Loire Valley

Salamander, emblem of François I

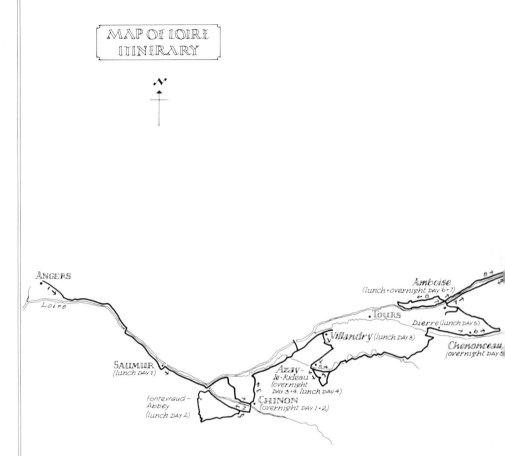

MAP OF LOIRE
ITINERARY

N

ANGERS

Loire

AMBOISE
(lunch + overnight DAY 6 + 7)

TOURS

Dierre (lunch DAY 5)

Villandry (lunch DAY 3)

Chenonceau
(overnight DAY 5

SAUMUR
(lunch DAY 1)

Azay-
le-Rideau
(overnight
DAY 3 + 4, lunch DAY 4)

Fontevraud-
Abbey
(lunch DAY 2)

CHINON
(overnight DAY 1 + 2)

———————— Main Route
- - - - - - - - Alternative Route to avoid Orléans

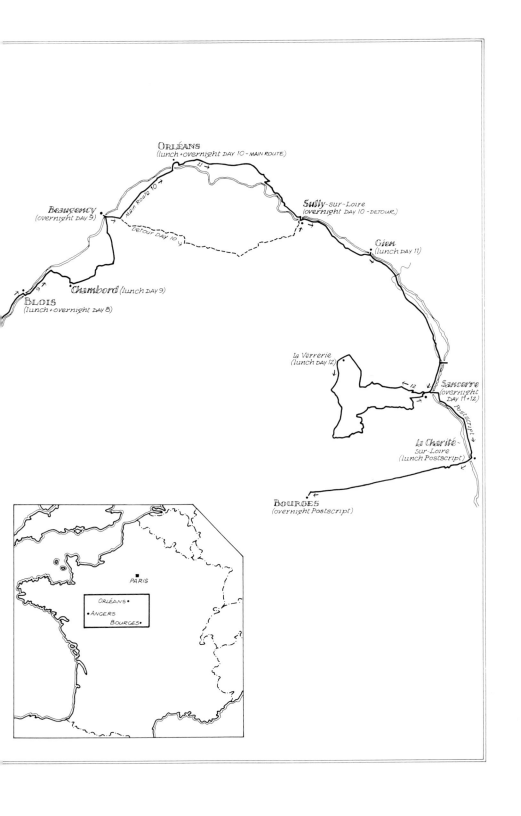

Le Gerbier de Jonc, the source of the Loire in Ardèche

Geography and Climate

Quite rightly the area is known as the 'Garden of France', and I have endeavoured to look into the question of why the soil in the Loire valley is so conducive to the growing of crops, why it has such fertile land.

Once the sea covered a large area of the region depositing a soft chalk which to this day can be seen on the banks of the rivers Cher, Vienne, Indre and Loir (not to be confused with the river Loire). This is known as the 'Tufa'. When the sea retreated it left the lakes you will see on your travels, and a great deal more limestone was deposited which is now covered by silt. The chalky deposits in the Sancerre area give the distinctive flavour to the region's wine. The resulting countryside contains a network of rivers with sandy banks. The silt of the Loire added to what today is one of the most fertile areas in the whole of France.

The Loire rises as a small stream, at the foot of Le Gerbier de Jonc in Ardèche. As it passes through the Massif Central it gathers speed and runs through deep valleys and gorges, by the time it reaches the Val de Loire it has spread out into a wide gentle looking river with islands and sandy banks. The current is still fast flowing and can be treacherous, it is therefore advisable to swim only where there are areas designated for safe bathing. The current can make you feel like an Olympic swimmer as it carries you along.

In winter this hospitable looking river changes character. It spreads out and deepens causing dangerous whirlpools and uprooting trees along its banks.

The Loire is the longest river in France, 627 miles long. The Val de Loire covers 240 miles. It passes through countryside ranging from flat to undulating, with outcrops of rock on which many of the châteaux were built.

There are vineyards all along the valley, on the gently sloping hillsides. Touraine is renowned for its orchards. Throughout the valley sunflowers are cultivated for their oil. The fields are very large, without hedges, for the growing of wheat, maize and rape.

However, there are still vast areas of forest, which are well managed. Fortunately forest fires are not as prevalent as they are in the south. The forests offer a rich supply of wood and are still full of game and wild life.

The valley also has its large industrial areas as well as a number of nuclear power stations, but pollution of the river is carefully monitored.

There are no great extremes of climate in the Loire valley throughout the year, although in July and August it can be very hot. I love May and June when the countryside is looking so beautifully green, the vineyards are coming to life, and for me the temperature is just about right. The Loire in September is much like England weatherwise and as autumn approaches you have the same wonderful colours of the season; this is when the grape-picking takes place. Winters can be pretty cold, but there is not a lot of snow. As the winds often come down the valley from the sea, they bring very cold clear air in their wake, and lovely cooling breezes in the summer. February and March can be damp and wet, but spring starts even earlier than in the Channel Islands, so this area produces many vegetables in advance of the main season.

Agriculture and Industry

Throughout the Loire valley you will find a predominance of vines, they are everywhere, and are a big source of employment. In the main wine producing areas, you will find at least one member of every family is working in the vineyard. The land also produces a wealth of vegetables and cereals, the west being one of the biggest suppliers of grain in the centre of France.

In the east around Saumur you will find strawberries, some of the best in France, blackcurrants, apricots, and walnuts — from which are made the world-renowned oil. Unexpectedly melons grow here in profusion. They were introduced to the region by the head gardener of Charles VIII, so they have been established for a long time. The Loire is generally considered the kitchen garden for Paris, providing a rich source of vegetables including asparagus (fat and succulent), french beans and, of course, mushrooms. As you travel through the centre of the valley you will see many large greenhouses producing lettuce and tomatoes.

The valley is well known for its flowers, everywhere you will see houses with their window boxes overflowing, and ever-popular pots of geraniums. You will also come across commercial growers with fields bursting with blooms for the markets.

As for the livestock, from the goat herds in the east of the valley come a large goat cheese industry. You will also see plenty of pigs for the area is well-known for its pork. The milk production comes from the large white Maine-Anjou cows.

Heavy industry hardly exists except around large towns like Tours and Orléans. In the smaller towns there are local industries such as porcelain in Gien.

There are several nuclear power stations in the valley, they are a blot on the landscape, but this does not worry the French as much as the English. They have learnt to live with it, with a view towards cheaper electricity, and of course, it is a terrific reservoir for local labour.

History

At one time the river Loire was considered to be the most strategically important river in the whole of France. In the Middle Ages French Kings were forever struggling with their feudal warlords. In Paris they felt out of touch, whereas the Loire valley was the geographical centre so here the great fortresses were built. For many periods during France's history, it not only became the favourite residential area for royalty, but also the centre of government. It was the heart and backbone of the country.

As you drive through the valley of the Loire, the many châteaux stand as the physical remains of the Royal Houses of France, and all the very great families who lived in and visited that area. A history of the Loire is therefore a history of the machinations for power within the French royalty and the great houses constantly aspiring to the power of the throne.

The Kings of France took advantage of the local population, by employing a lot of people as builders, cooks, servants, guards, stonemasons and the best craftsmen of the age, as well as artists, whose paintings today give us a clear picture of what life was like at the time.

These majestic châteaux have very fortunately been saved for us to revel in their history, they are exhilarating and in the majority of cases completely breathtaking, whether they are of early design built for defence or in the more ornate renaissance style.

During the time of the Revolution the area suffered very badly, it was the scene of many bloody battles and indiscriminate looting. In the Second World War the Loire valley was the centre of some of the worst fighting, towns such as Gien were partially destroyed and many bridges bombed. In 1944 came the liberation which was achieved by the American Army and those very brave men and women of the Resistance.

Today all the châteaux have been restored to their old glory, towns virtually rebuilt and, in many cases, new bridges built in place of the original ones.

You will find that I have discussed the history of certain areas in more detail as you follow the itinerary.

Joan of Arc

Joan of Arc was a peasant girl from Domremy which lies between Champagne and Lorraine. She was a pious child, who led a simple hardworking life at home with her brothers and sister. At the age of 13 she began to hear voices from God and St Michael, St Catherine and St Margaret.

The crown of France was in dispute between the Dauphin Charles, son of Charles VI, and the English King Henry VI, whose armies, in alliance with the Burgundians, occupied a large area in the northern part of France.

Guided by her voices, in May 1428 when she was only 16, Joan went to Vaucouleurs and asked for permission to meet the Dauphin. She was not taken seriously and returned to Domremy. She went back to Vaucouleurs in January of the following year. This time her sincerity was respected and her visions provoked interest.

Dressed in men's clothes, she travelled to Chinon, where she gained an audience with the Dauphin. Although he hid himself amongst his courtiers, she made straight for him and told him that she wished to lead his army against the English, so that he could be crowned at Reims. It was five years since his father's death, and he still had not been crowned.

Joan was interrogated by ecclesiastical authorities in Chinon and again in Poitiers, because of the fear of heresy. She told them that she would prove her mission at Orléans, which was being besieged by the English. In view of the desperate situation they sent a positive report to the King. She returned to Chinon and thence to Tours where she was joined by her brothers Jean and Pierre. She was provided with her own standard and banner. Joan said that her sword would be found in the Church of St Catherine-de-Fierbois and one was discovered there.

In April troops were mustered at Blois and they set out for Orléans. On arrival she was told to wait for reinforcements, but on May 4th she announced that they must attack. She revived the fighting spirit of the French and although she was wounded she carried on and within four days the English capitulated. Joan returned to Tours and urged the Dauphin to make haste to Reims for his coronation. After hesitating, it was decided to clear the English from other towns along the Loire, they attacked Beaugency after which she rejoined the Dauphin at Sully-sur-Loire.

In June the army assembled at Gien, where at last they set out for Reims pausing on the way at Loches, where Joan urged Charles on again. His coronation took place in the cathedral on July 17th. The Duke of Burgundy was in possession of Paris, but instead of attacking it, Charles VII returned to the Loire. Joan became impatient and set off for Paris, eventually Charles joined her in September. When they attacked Joan was wounded and yet the next day she sought to renew the attack but she was ordered to retreat.

They returned to Gien and later to Bourges. About this time she laid siege to La Charité-sur-Loire, but after a month they had to abandon it for lack of supplies. Joan rejoined the King who was spending the winter in the châteaux along the Loire.

In the spring of 1430, the Duke of Burgundy set out to attack Compiegne, so Joan left the King and set off with her brother Pierre and a small troop to come to their aid. She entered Compiegne under the cover of darkness and led a sortie, twice repelling the Burgundians, but was eventually surrounded by English reinforcements. Her troop retreated, but she stayed on until the last while the troops crossed the Oise river. Joan was captured and taken to the château in Vermandois. She tried to escape and was transferred to another château, where she jumped from the top of a tower into the moat. Her travels continued for she was then taken to Arras.

The Bishop of Beauvais asked that she should be handed over in the name of the English King for payment of 10,000 francs. Joan's trial was fixed to take place in Rouen. She was imprisoned in the château of Bouvieuil, which was occupied by the Earl of Warwick and later taken to the prison in Rouen, where she was brought to trial in order to show that Charles VII was a fool in the hands of a witch and that her behaviour showed blasphemous presumption.

Joan became ill and was attended by doctors, since the Earl of Warwick did not want her to die before the trial ended. Accusations and interrogations continued and she was threatened with torture. She asked if she could appeal to Rome, but her request was ignored.

Having been tried by a Church court,she was handed over to secular authorities for punishment, this being the English custom. Joan was burnt at the stake on May 30th, 1431.

Joan was canonized by Pope Benedict XV on May 16th, 1920. A national festival is held in her honour every year on the second Sunday in May.

Chronological Table of the Kings of France

(12th century to the Revolution)

	Came to the Throne
Philippe II (Philippe-Auguste)	1180
Louis VIII	1223
Louis IX (Saint Louis)	1226
Philippe III	1270
Philippe IV (Philippe-le-Bel)	1285
Louis X	1314
Jean I	1316
Philippe V	1316
Charles IV	1322

All the Valois Kings were descended from the brother of Philippe III.

Philippe VI (1328-50)
His reign saw the outbreak of the Hundred Years' War. Probably the most famous defeat for this King was at the Battle of Crecy, when the English archers fired arrows as 'thick as snow' and brought the French knights crashing to their deaths.

Jean II (1350–64)

This King was captured by the English. When he was released to raise a ransom, one of the hostages held in his place escaped and Jean felt honour bound to return to London where he died at the Savoy palace.

Charles V (1364–80)

Known as Charles the Wise. His reign was punctuated with skirmishes with the English and the King of Navarre. He was admired for his political and cultural achievements. He planned a magnificent library in the Louvre and completed the château in Vincennes.

Charles VI (1380–1422)

He was prey to fits of madness and his reign was marked by insubordination from the nobility. Again this French King suffered a crippling defeat against a smaller army at the Battle of Agincourt.

Charles VII (1422–61)

He was pale, thin and a trifle weedy. As the Dauphin he wanted to be left alone in his palace. He was stirred into action by Joan of Arc, who helped him to raise the siege of Orléans in 1429, but he abandoned her to the English in 1431.

By 1453 the English had been driven out of France (except Calais). The French Kings were at last masters in their own land.

Louis XI (1461–83)

Born in Bourges and spent his childhood in Loches. He was ruthless and devout, an intelligent and cunning diplomat. Louis XI was a tireless worker. He encouraged Guilds and industry. He introduced silk making to Lyons and Tours and initiated Rouen's commerce with England and printing at the Sorbonne.

There was a continuous struggle with the Burgundians, Edward IV of England and Charles the Bold, who was killed in the Battle of Nancy and peace followed. Charles the Bold's daughter married the Austrian Archduke Maximilian. Their daughter married Louis XI's son, and their son became Charles VIII. Louis XI died at the age of 60 at Plessis-les-Tours in the Touraine.

Charles VIII (1483–98)

Only 12 years of age when he became King, contemporaries describe him as small, ill formed with an ugly face, large, lustreless, short-sighted eyes and a large nose and thick lips. He also suffered from a stutter and a twitch.

In order to gain control of Brittany, he married Duchess Anne of Brittany. Charles saw himself as the last crusader and longed to fight the infidel and be crowned Emperor in Constantinople. He involved France in a series of wars in Italy. He died after hitting his head on a low door at the château in Amboise.

Louis XII (1498–1515)

The Valois-Orléans King, he was descended from Louis d'Orléans, brother of Charles VI.

Louis took as his second wife the widow of Charles VIII, Anne of Brittany, after brutally discarding his first wife. He became known as the 'father of his people' and during his reign France enjoyed economic growth and internal peace. In his old age he married Mary Tudor, sister of Henry VIII of England.

François I (1515–47)

The first of the Valois-Orléans Kings to descend from the third son of Louis d'Orléans.

François was fun-loving, flamboyant and authoritarian. He patronised the arts using Leonardo da Vinci and Celini to work on the châteaux of Fontainbleau, Blois and Chambord. He was captured by the Holy Roman Emperor and had to be ransomed.

Henri II (1547–59)

The second son of François I. Henri was held in Spain as a hostage for his father. He married Catherine de Medici but was dominated by his famous mistress, Diane de Poitiers.

François II (1559–60)

Eldest and sickly son of Henri II. Married Mary Queen of Scots.

Charles IX (1560–74)

He was only 10 years of age when he came to the throne, and was dominated by his mother Catherine de Medici who ruled as Regent. This sad and sickly boy was persuaded to back the massacre of Protestants on St Bartholomew's Eve. He died of tuberculosis.

Henri III (1574–89)

Youngest son of Henri II and the favourite son of Catherine de Medici. This intelligent and artistic King was notorious for his cruelty (he was said to have wrung the necks of his pet birds) and his boy friends upon whom he lavished presents. After murdering the Duke of Guise, Henri was himself murdered by a Dominican Friar.

Henri IV (1589–1610)

The first of the Bourbon Kings descended from the sixth son of Louis IX. This Protestant Henri of Navarre was known as 'Vert Gallant'. He is said to have exclaimed 'Paris is worth a Mass', before he was converted to Roman Catholicism in order to consolidate his position. Apart from ending the French Wars of Religion and reconstructing France, Henri found time to have at least 56 mistresses before being stabbed by a Roman Catholic schoolmaster when his coach was caught in a Paris traffic jam.

Louis XIII (1610–43)

His reign was most noted for his appointment of Cardinal Richelieu, and he saw the foundation of France's most glorious and stable period.

Louis XIV (1643–1715)

Known as the 'Sun King'. He was gifted, handsome and healthy. He took himself and his position seriously. He married Maria Theresa of Spain and had many mistresses, by whom he had eleven children. In later life he secretly married Françoise de Maintenon, who had brought up his illegitimate children.

The architectural style of this period is all pervasive at Versailles, the Opera and the Louvre.

The last years of Louis XIV's reign were marked by humiliation abroad, economic crisis at home, high taxation, bad harvest, famine and disease, all of which encouraged riots. His only legitimate son died followed by his two grandsons, the third grandson was already King of Spain, so he was succeeded by his great-grandson Louis XV.

Louis XV (1715–74)

Although apparently handsome, dignified and gracious, Louis XV was also indolent, self-indulgent and he filled his days with 'Wine, Women and Hunting'. His most famous mistresses were the Marquise de Pompadour and the Countess du Barry. These ladies and their friends controlled all the court appointments. Meanwhile unrest amongst the people continued to increase.

By the end of his reign France's glorious years were over. The ancient regime stood on the brink of revolution.

Louis XVI (1774–93)

He married Marie Antoinette daughter of the Holy Roman Emperor Francis I and Maria Theresa. He was heavy, short sighted, pious and virtuous. Louis XVI lacked the steel and intelligence needed to meet the crisis that was looming. He was dominated by his frivolous wife, who warped what judgement Louis had. Financial crisis, social unrest and political pressures led to the downfall of this King who bowed his head to Madame Guillotine on the 21st January 1793.

House of Guise

This was an influential Roman Catholic family in France during the sixteenth-century Wars of Religion.

Claude of Lorraine amassed a fortune. He was made Duc de Guise and a Peer of the Realm. His brother Jean was the Cardinal of Lorraine, and his eldest son Claude, who succeeded as Duc de Guise in 1550, was a prominent soldier. It was he who captured Calais from the English.

The Wars of Religion were fought between the Huguenots and the Roman Catholics. There was an emergence of the Protestant faith all over Europe, with the Lutherans in Germany, Elizabeth in England and the Calvinists in France, whereas in Spain and the Spanish Netherlands the Catholic Inquisition was burning heretics. Many atrocities were carried out in the name of religion. The influence of the Guise family rivaled that of the ruling Valois family, and they took the opportunity of the religious upheaval to seize more power. After marrying their niece, Mary (Queen of Scots) to the Dauphin, they challenged the influence of Catherine de Medici.

In 1560 the Huguenots and Bourbons attempted a coup d'état against the Guises in Amboise, with horrendous results. Their bodies were hung from the battlements, and some were thrown alive in sacks into the Loire. Henri Duc de Guise took part in the infamous Massacre of St Bartholomew's Day in Paris. In 1576 he formed the Holy League of Catholic Nobles, known as the Catholic League.

In the name of the Wars of Religion, Henri Duc de Guise won two victories over the Huguenots and became Lieutenant General of the Realm. He had a powerful following, but was denied the final victory. Henri III sensed that his throne was in danger and decided to do away with him. On Christmas Eve 1588, Henri Duc de Guise was murdered in the château at Blois. His ashes were thrown into the Loire. A painting of the assassination can be seen in the château.

Within the year, Catherine de Medici died and Henri III was also murdered. Henri of Navarre (the Evergreen Gallant) became Henri IV, and the Wars of Religion ceased.

The House of Valois

This was the royal house of France from 1328-1589. The Valois Kings ruled during the transition from the feudal system to the early modern period, when France became a unified nation state.

This began with the Hundred Years' War, which broke out in the reign of Philip VI, 1328-50. He fought against the English and feudal lords such as Amagnac and the Burgundians. Charles VII (1422-61) continued to restore Royal power by trying to establish the crown's exclusive right to employ an army and to levy taxes. Louis XI (1461-83) carried on the work of establishing royal rule throughout France. The house of Valois continued through the reigns of Charles VIII, Louis XII, François I and Henri II but with Henri III (1574-89) the Valois dynasty ended as there was no heir.

Henry IV was the first King of the House of Bourbon.

The Medici Family

The Medicis were an Italian family of bankers that ruled Florence and later Tuscany.

From 1434-1737, they were a powerful family, who provided the Church with three Popes. They were prominent patrons of the arts, and married into the royal families of France. Although they ruled like monarchs, they were not royal, but their great wealth was welcome as dowries for both Catherine de Medici, who married Henry II, and Marie de Medici who became the second wife of Henry IV.

Plantagenet

This was the surname used by members of the royal house of England, between 1154-1485. They were descendants of Geoffrey Count of Anjou and Matilda, daughter of the English King, Henry I. The derivation comes from the Latin 'genista', meaning broom. It is said to have begun as a nickname, because Count Geoffrey wore a sprig of broom in his hat and planted broom on his land to improve the cover for hunting.

Henry Plantagenet, Count of Anjou, was ruler of vast areas of France, before he became King Henry II of England. He inherited Normandy from his mother and Anjou, Maine and Touraine from his father. When he married Eleanor of Aquitaine he also ruled over an area from Bayonne across to the Auvergne. After his succession he acquired Brittany as well.

Henry and the sons who succeeded him were known as the Angevin Kings (the adjectival form of the house of Anjou). His sons maintained their ties with France, by marrying French wives. Richard I (the Lion Heart) married Berengaria of Navarre and John married Isabella of Angoulême, John's son Henry III married Eleanor of Provence.

Edwards I,II and III were also Kings of the Plantagenet dynasty, and the last claimant to the Plantagenet heritage was Henry VI, by the end of his reign the only French territory left in English hands was Calais.

Châteaux

Château is directly translated as castle and indeed the ones built in the 13th and 14th centuries are similar in style to our English castles, because in both cases the design was dictated by considerations of defence. Later châteaux retained the trimmings of defence for grandeur, but they became private residences on a grand scale and took on a unique French appearance, with their many turrets and fine decoration.

The Gothic châteaux were fortifications built around a courtyard. They were planned to withstand a seige and were usually built on a hill with a commandng view of the river or countryside. They have very thick battlemented walls, interspersed with round towers with narrow windows and topped with machicolations, these are openings through a parapet for dropping missiles onto the enemy below. A moat and drawbridge provided further protection.

The 15th century brought a decline in the feudal system and changes in methods of warfare. Nobles began building luxurious country houses, such as Azay-le-Rideau and Chenonceaux. The sites were not chosen with defence in mind (a hill, or the edge of the Loire) instead the châteaux were placed on tributaries in this now popular area of the Loire valley. The designs retained the characteristics of fortification with the added elegance and comfort provided by the architects of the Renaissance.

La Charité-sur-Loire, from the ramparts

The Epicure's Guide

Ermine, emblem of Anne of Brittany

Food

The Loire valley covers an enormous area, embracing Anjou, Touraine and Sologne. The food of the region is influenced by the river, with all its fresh fish, and the extremely fertile soil, that is why it is known as the Garden of France. Because of its mild climate many early vegetables and fruits are cultivated. The numerous caves along the banks of the river in the Saumur area are used for the cultivation of mushrooms. There are also some unusual wild mushrooms available in their season.

The great forests still supply plenty of game, which inspire many casserole dishes, in whose variety the region excells.

As you would expect in the western area, nearer the coast, the local specialities are sea food dishes, oysters, mussels, crayfish and a great variety of other shellfish. The west has a well known sauce called 'Beurre Blanc', ask for this as it is a wonderful complement for fish. Eels are very popular and are caught at the mouth of the Loire, and also in the river itself. Just recently I was fortunate enough to catch eels in the Loire in the morning, these were cooked in time for lunch with white wine, herbs and shallots accompanied with a fresh salad. It was a meal fit for a king.

In Touraine a favourite dish is young ducklings cooked in their own juices, and served with a sauce of cherries and port wine, plus local-grown vegetables such as leeks and baby turnips.

Cheeses in the west are many, the most famous being Port Salut, and Fromage du Curé (it was first made by a monk). I must mention rabbit in cider, another favourite dish in this region. You will find a lot of rabbit dishes in the Loire valley, obviously there are plenty of them in the vast, frequently almost empty, expanse of countryside.

Moving to the east of the region during your travels you will find some of the finest food in the whole of France. Pork is a predominant dish — pork chops with prunes are delicious. Their sausages are out of this world, try andouillettes and potted pork, or pork sausage stuffed with the meat of a chicken, this makes an excellent starter. Another favourite is 'steak au poivre' peppered steak to us, which is so different to what we are used to. You can even obtain good quality tins of the sauce to take home for yourself and your friends. The ingredients include: green peppers, cream, white wine and cognac. Another favourite found in the river Loire are small fish not dissimilar to whitebait known as 'friture de la Loire', served with bread and lemon, it is quite succulent. Talking of fish the Loire gives us salmon, trout and pike. Pike is hardly ever eaten in England but here it is a delicacy. The secret is that it must be very fresh, it may be poached in a court bouillon with white wine and accompanied by beurre blanc sauce.

Walnut oil is manufactured in the upper Loire valley, buy some before you return home as it is quite inexpensive. Many salads are dressed with walnut oil, the nutty flavour blends well, especially with tomatoes.

Another popular vegetable you will meet are mushrooms cooked in every possible way, my favourite is les champignons farcis à la crème, this being mushrooms with a cream sauce.

In the east of the region, you will see herds of large dark brown goats grazing in the fields. Their milk is used to make a variety of cheeses. The small cheeses, Crottin de Chevre, translated 'Goats' Droppings' can be obtained in different stages of maturity, soft and white or hard blue and very strong. At this stage they need to be washed down with plenty of Sancerre blanc. Do try the fromage blanc made from goat's milk, and accompanied with strong shallots, nobody will speak to you for ages, but it is worth a few hours of silence.

Why not try snails, garnished with butter and garlic (the famous escargots)? Lots of people are put off by the mere fact of them being snails, but try them, they are super. One summer morning, when there had been a light shower during the night, we went out and collected some. We had to leave them for a few days to cleanse and then cooked them. They made a meal in themselves with freshly baked bread. Snails are available throughout the region. Indeed these days many are imported from China!

There are plenty of local melons, plums and wild strawberries, apricots and pears. Try a 'Tart Tartin', a toffee-flavoured apple tart. Sunday is a big day in France as far as food is concerned, watch what the locals buy, you will see Tart Tartin coming out of the shops in every possible size. Patisseries may at first appear very expensive, but not when you examine the quality.

Please try and visit a market, most towns have one, you will see all the local food from the area displayed. Watch the locals buying live chickens for coq au vin. You will also see many different types of bread as well as the popular long sticks. By standing and watching you will find out much more than I can tell you in this book. One of the highlights of my stay in France during the summer is to visit the market and buy all the fresh produce to last several days.

I would just like to say a few words about the eating habits of the French. I often get asked 'is it true you hang on to your knife and fork after the first dish?' Well this used to be the habit, and you will still find it in smaller country restaurants, but not in larger establishments. The only time a Frenchman eats butter is usually with the hors d'oeuvres, and you do not get butter served with your cheese unless you ask for it. The normal practice is to serve a salad separate from your main dish, if you wish to have it with it, just ask the waiter, this sometimes applies to vegetables as well. Recently in Gien I ordered a great pork dish and a tomato salad, the salad arrived, and I carried on talking to my wife, after about 15 minutes I noticed the serving staff standing waiting and realised they were hoping I would consume the salad so they could serve the main dish, a small point but it may help you.

Breakfast is only to see you through to lunch. Very rarely, even in the biggest hotel, will they cook you a full English breakfast, just plenty of good hot coffee, bread and a selection of jams. To watch once an American gentleman trying to order a hard boiled egg by sign language was a sight for sore eyes, extremely amusing, my wife came to his rescue but I do not know if it ever arrived.

In all the years that I have been visiting France I have yet to have a good cup of tea, they just do not make it to fit English tastes. Take some with you and make your own if you can, but the coffee is great. When you ask for coffee in a café you will always get a small cup of pretty strong black coffee, ask specifically for 'café au lait' or in my case a 'grand café au lait' if you want milk.

How the French love their food. You are expected to enjoy it and you must devote at least 1½ to 2 hours for lunch, and the same for dinner, this is the custom. I go to a little village restaurant every Sunday where 2 to 2½ hours is quite common. The French know how to cook, and how to present food, long may it last. Frozen food, especially vegetables, are hardly known in the Loire valley, but I did see, early one morning as I was going to collect my bread, a frozen food van outside a Michelin recommended restaurant delivering frozen chips. I hope and pray this will never catch on in a big way, and somehow I do not think it will, especially in the country areas, but this incident would be enough to make Escoffier turn in his grave.

Bon appetit.

Wine

The Loire valley is one of the major wine producing areas in France ranging across the wines of Muscadet, Anjou, Chinon, Azay-le-Rideau, Vouvray and of course Sancerre and Pouilly-Fumé. The valley's vineyards vary from the very small producer with a few hectares of land, to the extremely large, whose products are drunk by wine connoisseurs throughout the world.

I strongly believe that you should endeavour to drink the wine of the area you are visiting, unless you have tried it in the past and taken a dislike to that particular type. I have heard people ordering in Saumur and Sancerre, some well known brand of Burgundy or Bordeaux, and I shudder when I hear the word 'Chianti', not that I have got anything against these wines, but they do this to be on the safe side, unless you try the local wines you will never know what they are like. They are of course cheaper when consumed in the area where they are produced. Let me now give you a short tour around the principle wine growing areas.

Let us start in the west around the Muscadet region, one of the most well known everyday drinking wines in France. It is amazing to think that when I first visited France after the war, Muscadet was considered to be the 'vin ordinaire' usually drunk in the cheapest of cafés, today it is ranked as one of the top wines, and it is still remarkably inexpensive.

It is produced in the region around Nantes (not actually part of this tour but still in the Loire valley). The grape is mainly of Melon de Bourgogne but the locals named it Muscadet and this has stuck. Interestingly this is one of the earliest grapes to be harvested, usually late August to early September. The town of

Nantes is the centre of the area, and is in Brittany, perhaps one day you will visit it, a lovely place, excellent hotels, and wow, the fish especially the oysters are the best in France, and accompanied by Muscadet, what could be better?

Next stop on the wine tour is Saumur (see Day 1). The wines of this part are known as Anjou, the best known is Cabernet Rosé d'Anjou, which you can buy in most chain wine stores in the UK. I believe the best wine produced in Saumur is the red. The white wines have something in common with the German wines, which are so easy to drink and carry on drinking without too much effect. The grape that is used for the white is Chenin Blanc the French call it Pineau de la Loire and that for the red is Cabernet-Franc and Cabernet-Sauvignon. The vineyards are some of the most northerly in France, so that climate plays a very important part in the success of its production. Undoubtedly Anjou is best known for its sweet and rosé wines, and the most famous area is the Coteaux du Layon.

Wine producers you can visit in the area:

Domaine Cady
Pierre and Philippe Cady
Valette, St Aubin-de-Luigne
49190 Rochefort-Sur-Loire
Tel: (41) 78 33 69
Open – daily from 9.0am until 8.0pm. No appointment needed.
This house produces an excellent red wine.
Note: Rochefort-Sur-Loire lies southwest of Angers, at the start of the Coteaux du Layon.

Clos Coulaine
François Roussier
Coulaine
Tel: (41) 72 21 06
Open – Monday to Friday: 10.0am until noon and 2.0pm until 6.0pm; Saturday: 10.0am until noon. No appointment needed.
Again, a very good red wine.

Domaine De La Croix Des Loges
Christian Bonnin
49540 Matigne-Briand
Tel: (41) 59 43 66

Open – Monday to Saturday: 9.0am until noon and 3.0pm until 7.0pm. It is closed during the month of October. No appointment needed.
Good range of white wines and rosé, and Saumur Mousseux the first class sparkling wine.

For further wine information:
Maison du Vin de l'Anjou
5 Place Kennedy
Angers
and at
Maison du Vin de Saumur
25 Rue Beaurepaire
Saumur

Now we enter the Touraine for the red wines of Chinon and Bourgeuil, with small vineyards around Azay-le-Rideau. (Try these at your hotel in Azay-le-Rideau.) I believe these wines are underrated. I personally think that Chinon is a lovely wine which complements the best of food. You will hear it said that it is a bad traveller: what a load of codswallop. I bring it home, and lay it down, great stuff. The grape is mainly Cabernet-Franc.

Wine producers you can visit in the area:

Domaine René Couly
12 Rue Diderot
37502 Chinon
Tel: (47) 93 05 84
This is close to your hotel in Chinon, but you have to book an appointment, contact Couly Dutheil.

Jean Claude Bodin
Le Bergeonniere St-Romain
41440 Noyers-Sur-Cher
Tel: (54) 71 70 43
Open – daily 8.0am until noon and 2.0pm until 6.0pm. No appointment needed.

Guy Deletang et Fils
Guy Deletang
St Martin-le-Beau
37270 Montlouis
Tel: (47) 50 67 25
Open – daily 10.0am until noon and 2.0pm until 6.0pm. No appointment
needed.

Le Clair Père et Fils
La Foltiere
Ange
41400 Montrichard
Tel: (54) 32 09 72

Even though Vouvray is a Touraine wine I want to keep it separate, in a class of its
own.

A lovely wine, again the Chenin Blanc grape, but compared to the Anjou variety,
it is sweeter. Some people say it has a honey flavour, well whatever it has it is
good. I always feel the people of Vouvray are proud of their wine, and they show
it, not only in its presentation but the proof is in the drinking. The sparkling
wines of Vouvray are very well known, and the beauty is that they can be drunk
very young (why keep it hanging about). It is wonderful with fish and goat's
cheese. I am not going to recommend a supplier in Vouvray, there are so many
small producers it would be hard to pick one out. Enjoy yourself in Vouvray,
great people and great wine. Henri IV owned vineyards in Vouvray, he must
have been a man with a lot of taste because he reserved all the production for his
own personal consumption, how about that for a recommendation.

This may be a good place in this book to advise you to buy your wines from the
producers as you travel on this tour. Don't wait until you return on the boat, it is
much cheaper to buy this way, and most of all if you buy it in France, you can
bring more home. Get a leaflet on the boat before you start your journey, it will
tell you all about it, and also should you bring back more than your allowance,
declare it at the Customs. What you will have to pay is far less when added to the
purchase price than you would have to pay for an equivalent wine in England.
Certainly worth thinking about.

Now my dear readers we have arrived on our wine tour in Sancerre. Ah, Sancerre, the King of Wines! Sancerre is produced from the Sauvignon grape, and grows on the chalky hills around the town. This gives it a flavour of its own, very distinctive, it is usually referred to as having a Gunflint flavour by the experts. The locals also love their Sancerre red, which they are rather inclined to keep to themselves. This is made from the Pinot Noir grape. Sancerre should be drunk when young, it is not the best wine to be kept for any length of time. Excellent with goat's cheese, and sea food, especially oysters.

Pouilly-Fumé is made from the same Sauvignon grape, but grown on different soil, this gives it the delicious smoky flavour which it is so well known for. Do not confuse this wine with Pouilly-Fuisse, also a white wine but from the Mâcon area in Burgundy. Two wine producers well worth visiting are:

Domain Balland-Chapuis
Owner Joseph Balland
Chapuis BP 24
Bué
18300 Sancerre
Tel: (48) 54 06 67
You must make an appointment. In the village of Bué there are also many other small producers worth visiting.

Serge Montagu
St. Gemme
This is a small village just outside Sancerre. My wife, incidentally, designed the label for this producer.

As you enter Sancerre you will see a sign to the Caves de la Mignonne. These are worth seeing, and you can sample wines and obtain information. Major wine festivals are held in these caves, which cover a vast area.

Always buy your wine (if you are buying 6 bottles or more) direct from the producer, and not from the shops, unless you just want the odd bottle. The producer will pack them well for your journey home.

Bon Santé!

Handy Tips

HOW TO GET THERE FROM THE UK
The Itinerary begins at Angers; most people use the car ferry services (detailed below) and drive direct to Angers. Do book early if you are travelling in the summer months or over a bank holiday.

Brittany Ferries
Portsmouth to St Malo: crossing 9 hours; Portsmouth to Caen: crossing 5½ to 6½ hours; Plymouth to Roscoff: crossing 6 hours; Poole to Cherbourg: crossing 4½ hours (summer only). I have found that the night crossing to St Malo is very good, you have a splendid dinner on board, sleeping in a comfortable cabin as you travel overnight, and you arrive fresh in the morning. You can then get to the start of your tour very quickly. On your return journey you can stay in the lovely town of St Malo and catch a morning boat to Portsmouth.

Sealink Dieppe Ferries
Newhaven to Dieppe: crossing 4 hours. There is a convenient ferry timed at 10am arriving in Dieppe at 3pm. After lunch on board, take a short drive to Rouen, where you stay overnight and head for Angers the following morning.

P & O European Ferries
Portsmouth to Le Havre: crossing 5½ hours (day), 7-8 hours (night); Dover to Calais: crossing 1¼ hours; Dover to Boulogne: crossing 1 hour 40 mins.

Sealink
Portsmouth to Cherbourg: crossing 4¾ hours (day), 6 hours (night), this ferry only operates in the summer; Dover to Calais: crossing 1½ hours; Folkestone to Boulogne: crossing 1¾ hours.

Hoverspeed
Dover to Boulogne: crossing 40 mins.

Sally Line
Ramsgate to Dunkirk: crossing 2½ hours.

Air France operate from London to Paris, with connecting services to the valley. They have a fly/car scheme. Details from Air France, 158 New Bond Street, London W1Y 0AY, tel: (01) 499 8611.

French Railways operate a service from Paris to major towns in the Loire valley with hire car facilities. Details from SNCF, French Railways, 179 Piccadilly, London W1V 0BA. Hertz and Avis are represented in all major towns.

In the early 1990s, a new fast train will be operating from Paris to Tours, with connections to the channel ports.

Information can be obtained from the French Government Tourist Office, 178 Piccadilly, London W1V 0AL. Open Monday to Friday 9am-5pm. Tel: (01) 491 7622 (urgent enquiries); (01) 499 6911 (24-hour recorded information service).

CREDIT CARDS
Diners Club, American Express, Carte Bleu (Visa/Barclaycard) and Eurocard (Mastercard/Access) are usually accepted in hotels and restaurants, although it is always wise to check before entry. Some Autoroute petrol stations and restaurants accept them, again check. Hypermarkets do not usually accept them. Always check the amount that appears on the receipt when paying by cheque card, in France no decimal point is shown between FRANCS and CENTIMES.

It is wise to arrange with your bank in the UK to issue you with a Eurocheque facility, you will then have a 'Eurocheque' card and cheques which you can cash up to £100 in any major bank, on any one day. Most hotels will accept Eurocheques.

CURRENCY
If you take more than £1,200 (12,000FF) to France you must declare it.

DISABLED VISITORS
Just send a S.A.E. to the French Government Tourist Office, see above, they will send you a special information sheet.

DINING OUT
In France the population are inclined to eat early. You will notice that everything shuts down at lunchtime 12 noon until 2pm and dinner usually starts at 7pm.

Sunday is their great day out as far as restaurants are concerned. Try and book a table at least 24 hours ahead if at all possible. Note: many restaurants close on Sunday evenings. The beauty of France (and this is now catching on in the UK and USA) is that all restaurants display a set menu and à la carte menu outside. In France this is law, but it is wonderful to know before you enter roughly what the price of the evening will be.

TOURIST OFFICES
Each major town in the Loire valley has a Tourist Office (Office de Tourisme and Syndicats d'Initiative) and they will be available to advise you on restaurants, hotels, local entertainment, etc. Everywhere I have used these offices I have always found them extremely helpful.

WATER AND MILK
The water that is served in hotels and restaurants is perfectly safe to drink. You can buy pasteurised milk in all shops and major outlets.

BRITISH CONSULATES
You can find the nearest Consulate by referring to the telephone directory, but the police will always help you in contacting them.

ELECTRICITY
The electricity in the majority of France is 220 volt. Mainly 2 pin plugs are used, and I strongly advise you to take an adaptor with you, they are very cheap to buy, and usually can be purchased at AA and RAC Port Offices.

MEDICAL
If you are a British citizen check with your local DHSS office as you may be eligible for emergency cover under Form III. You can always get medical advice and first aid from pharmacies, and these you will recognise by their 'Green Cross'.

CUSTOMS ALLOWANCES
Obtain from your Ferry Office, Travel Agent, or Airport the Customs leaflet. This will show you what you can take into France and bring back to the UK. If you have a problem do not hesitate to contact the Customs Officers, who you will always find are helpful and prepared to offer advice, this can save you an awful lot of trouble, worry and anguish.

THE METRIC SYSTEM

2.2lbs	:	1 kilo
1¾ pints	:	1 litre
1 gallon	:	4.54 litres
1 mile	:	1.6 kilometres
5 miles	:	8 km

To convert Centigrade to Fahrenheit is roughly C x 2 plus 32.

PASSPORTS

If you are a British National you only need a valid passport. This can be either a full British passport valid up to ten years, or a British Visitor's passport which is valid for one year. You can, if you are only staying for a maximum of 60 hours, obtain from the British Post Office a British Excursion Document.

POST

You can always arrange for post to be sent to you for collection at a post office in France. These to be sent c/o Poste Restante, Poste Centrale in the town you will be visiting. You will need to show your passport when collecting and there is a very small fee.

MUSEUMS

On Sunday there are lower entrance fees for children, students and senior citizens. Museums are closed on Easter Sunday and Easter Monday, and Christmas Day and on Public Holidays; most National museums close on a Tuesday.

SHOP AND BANK OPENING HOURS

Banks are open 9am-noon, 2pm-4pm weekdays and are closed either on a Saturday or a Monday. Note: banks close early on the day before a bank holiday, usually at noon.

Post Offices: 8am-7pm weekdays and 8am-noon Saturdays. In smaller towns they close for lunch. Food shops: 7am-6.30/7.30pm. Other shops: 9am-6.30/ 7.30pm. You will find that many shops close all day or half day on a Monday. Some food shops especially bakers open on Sunday mornings. But as usual in France in small towns they always close at lunchtime from noon-2pm. Most supermarkets and hypermarkets stay open into the evening until 9/10pm Monday to Saturday. The majority close Monday mornings.

TELEPHONE
To dial the UK from France, first dial 19, wait until the continuous tone recurrs, then dial 44 followed by your STD code (minus the first 0) and then your number.

EMERGENCY NUMBERS
FIRE – 18
POLICE – 17
OPERATOR – 13
DIRECTORY ENQUIRIES – 12

You will find a lot of telephone booths now take phonecards (known as telecarte) you can buy them from Post Offices and certain shops which you will find advertised on the phone booths. If there is a 'Blue Bell Sign' you can receive calls.

MAPS
We recommend you use Michelin Maps 1/200,000 – 1cm:2km, nos 232 and 238 to accompany your tour. A complete map of the area is shown on pages 10-11.

Detailed maps of the itinerary are as follows:
Text map, days 1-2, p. 42
Text map, days 3-5, p. 74
Text map, days 6-9, p. 82
Text map, days 10-11, p. 118
Text map, days 12-postscript, p. 128
At the beginning of each day are listed the grid references of places visited on the route. Grid references are given longitude first, then latitude (i.e. reading from the perimeter of the map horizontally then vertically.)

Advice to Motorists

You should display a GB sign on the back of the car as near to the number plate as possible, and you *must* have a full valid driving licence and current insurance certificate. If the vehicle is not owned by you, a letter of authorisation from the owner is required. This particularly applies to Company Cars.

PETROL
You cannot obtain petrol coupons in France. Unleaded petrol is widely available in France (sans plomb). Should your car run on LPG gas, you can obtain a map from the French Government Tourist Office in London showing stockists.

MOTORWAYS
You will find garages open 24 hours and emergency telephones every 2km. The autoroutes are privately financed so therefore you have to pay a toll at intervals.

SPEED LIMITS
The French have two types of speed limit, one for dry roads and the other for wet.

WET ROADS	DRY ROADS	
110km	130km	per hour on toll motorways
100km	110km	per hour on dual carriageways and motorways without tolls
80km	90km	per hour on other roads
60km	60km	per hour in towns

Remember that when you enter a town or a village you will see the name sign; this is the start of the speed limit. As you leave you will see a bar through the name of the town or village and this means you are back to normal speed limits.

If you have just passed your test you cannot drive over 90km per hour during the first year. I would advise you to buy a sticker reading '90' which the French display. These can be obtained from garages, supermarkets, etc. This warns the following motorist so he will realise why you cannot go faster.

France has now introduced a new minimum speed limit of 80km per hour (50 miles per hour) for the outside lane of motorways during daylight hours, providing that you have good visibility and are on level ground.

I cannot emphasise more the need to drive within the speed limits. The French Police are very vigilant, and do remember you can be fined on the spot (and it is not cheap). The minimum fine for speeding is 1,300 francs which must be paid in cash, no cheques or credit cards.

DRINKING AND DRIVING
The French have random breath testing, and you are fined on the spot, if you exceed the drink/driving level, from 2,500FF to 5,000FF in cash.

PRIORITÉ À DROITE
In built up areas and towns, the priorité is still in operation, and you must give way to any vehicle coming out of a side-turning on the right. The rule no longer exists at roundabouts, however, therefore you give way to cars already on the roundabout as in England.

PLEASE NOTE THE FOLLOWING:
1) You cannot drive on an English provisional licence, even with 'L' plates.
2) The minimum age you are able to drive is 18.
3) Seat belts must always be worn by driver and front-seat passenger.
4) If your children are under ten years of age they cannot travel in the front of the car (unless you have not got a back seat).
5) If you must stop on a main road, always drive your car off the road.
6) When you meet a 'stop' sign, come completely to a halt. I have seen people booked for moving slowly at a 'stop' sign.
7) You must carry a triangular red warning sign, unless your car is fitted with hazard lights.
8) In poor visibility and at night always drive on dipped or full headlights.
9) It is essential (and law) that you carry a spare-bulb kit.
10) Your headlights should be adjusted to right-hand drive. You can buy black adhesive stickers to fit most headlights in this country before departure. If you are in France for any length of time have yellow-tinted headlights fitted.

All these 10 points are very important, if you do not abide by them the police can fine you on the spot.

See also Glossary of Motoring Terms, p. 156.

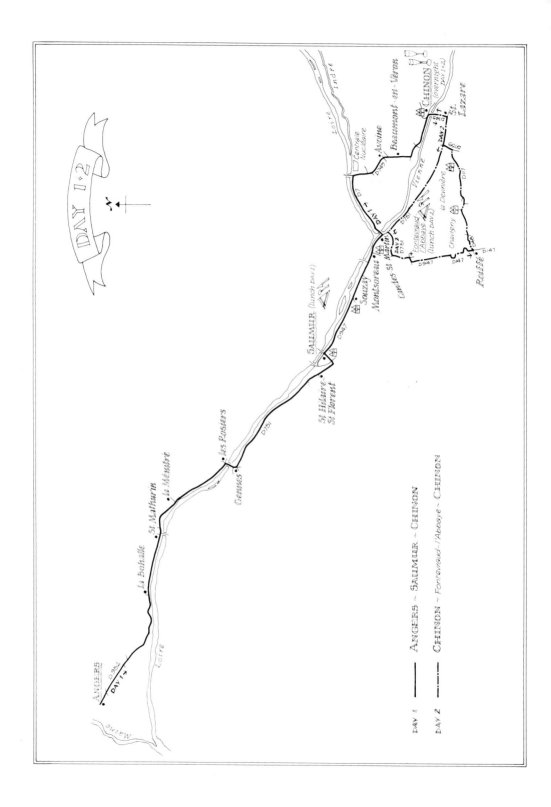

DAY 1·2

ANGERS

Maine

Loire

D952
DAY 1 →

La Bohalle

St Mathurin

la Ménitre

Blaison

D751

Gennes

les Rosiers

St Hilaire-
St Florent

D947

SAUMUR (lunch DAY 1)

Souzay
Montsoreau
candes St Martin

DAY 1

Loire

Indre

Centrale
Nucléaire

Avoine

Beaumont-en-Véron

CHINON
(overnight
DAY 1·2)

St
Lazare

D7

D751

D751
DAY 2
Fontevraud
l'Abbaye
(lunch DAY 2)

Vienne

la Deunière

Chavigny

D947

D47

Roiffé

D117

D47

DAY 2

——— ANGERS ~ SAUMUR ~ CHINON

—·—·— CHINON ~ Fontevraud - l'Abbaye ~ CHINON

DAY 1

DAY 2

The Itinerary

Porcupine, emblem of Louis XII

Arrival

The itinerary commences at Angers — I suggest you arrive in the town the evening before the tour commences.

USEFUL INFORMATION: ANGERS

Postal Address:	49000 Maine-et-Loire
Population:	150,000
Altitude:	20 M
Distances:	Paris 304 km, Blois 150 km, Orléans 225 km, Saumur 45 km
Railway Station:	Tel: (41) 88 50 50
Taxis:	Tel: (41) 87 76 00
Tourist Office:	Place Kennedy (just below the château) Tel: (41) 88 69 93. Open throughout the year
Annual events:	
March	Antiques fair
June	Festival of Angers
July	Festival of Angers (Concerts, theatre, and contemporary music)
September	Folklore festival
November	Autumn painting exhibition Flower market (Saturday mornings, in front of the Town Hall) Antique market (Place Imbach)

Hôtel de l'Univers
2 Place et 16 Rue de la Gare
49000 Angers
Tel: (41) 88 43 58

A very pleasant and extremely comfortable hotel, in the centre of town, close to the station. The bedrooms are well appointed. Unfortunately there is no restaurant, but there are many in the vicinity catering for most tastes. A warm and friendly atmosphere pervades throughout the hotel.

Open all year
Rooms: 45
Facilities: Bar, garage parking
Credit cards: all major cards
Rating: ★★

La Petite Marmite
Place de Gare
Angers

This small restaurant is just opposite the main railway station. It is run by a young husband and wife team, and has a very good menu. There is not a large choice but the food is well cooked and presented. Prices are good.

Rating: ★★

La Croix de Guerre
23 rue Château-Gontier
Angers
Tel: (41) 88 66 59

This is a very comfortable hotel, and is situated close to the Place Leroy.

Open all year
Rooms: 18
Facilities: Restaurant (*Relais Gastronomique*)
Credit cards: all major cards accepted
Rating: ★★

Château and garden at Angers

DAY 1

Angers, Saumur, Montsoreau, Chinon: approx. 80 km (50 miles).

Today your journey begins, but before setting off, you will spend the first part of the morning in Angers. There is much of interest to be seen, but endeavour to leave by 11.30 am. If the sun is shining brightly, I recommend a picnic for lunch. You will pass many well appointed picnic areas, on your journey, right beside the beautiful river Loire. Alternatively, lunch in Saumur, if you can get there in time.

In the afternoon, the road from Saumur to Chinon takes you away from the river Loire to the river Vienne at Montsoreau, and you follow a picturesque route into Chinon.

Overnight at Chinon.

Map references:
Angers	0°33'W 47°28'N
St Hilaire-St Florent	0°07'W 47°16'N
Saumur	0°05'W 47°16'N
Montsoreau	0°04'E 47°14'N
Chinon	0°14'E 47°10'N

Route shown p. 42.

Breakfast at Angers

Angers is the principal town of Anjou in the department of Maine-et-Loire, it is situated on the river Maine. At first glance you may feel as though you are in a characterless big city, but Angers has an atmosphere of its own, combining the old with the new, as it was very badly bombed in the 1939-45 war, and part of the town was completely rebuilt. Angers is a busy town, but do not be put off by its size and industry. It is the centre for many tourists who are visiting the châteaux in the west of the Loire.

You have so much to see during the morning. Your first call will be a visit to the château. It is a short walk so you can leave your car at the hotel if you wish, or park below the château. Every château in the Loire valley has its own character as you will find. The château of Angers is no exception. It stands majestically above the Maine river, with its seventeen stunted towers, the tops of which were destroyed in the 16th century, when there was an order to demolish the whole castle. Fortunately, this is as far as they got, when the order was rescinded. This was the home of the Counts of Anjou and served as the capital of the Plantagenets. The prime reason for visiting the château is not only to revel in its beauty and wonderfully laid out gardens, but to see the famous Musée des Tapisseries, the home of the world-renowned Apocalypse Tapestries (The Tentures de L'Apocalypse). One is immediately taken aback by their enormous size. It is well worth obtaining a guide leaflet in English. It is believed that they were ordered by Louis I of Anjou to decorate his château. Woven in 1375 by Nicolas Bataille, they follow the text of Revelations. They are considered to be some of the finest examples of this art to come down to us from the Middle Ages. The designer was Henequin de Bruges, who set out to illustrate sin and damnation in relation to the second advent. The tapestries stretched a distance of 335 ft when they were complete. At the time of the Revolution, they were thrown into the street. The citizens of the town took parts away to make carpets and covers. Two-thirds of the tapestries have now been recovered.

The château is open all the year, but the hours vary according to the season. During the summer it is open 9.30am-6pm without a break for lunch.

From the château you can walk through the old town which has beautiful, half-timbered houses — to the St Maurice Cathedral. I would not say that this is my favourite cathedral, but it is still worth a visit. It dates from the 12th/13th century. The stained glass windows are well worth seeing, these date from the

12th/16th century. Before leaving Angers you need to decide on your lunch plans. Either head swiftly to Saumur (30 miles) or collect a picnic from one of the many charcuterie. There is an excellent one only two doors from the Hôtel de l'Univers.

Take the D952 Route Touristique signposted to Saumur (avoid the N147), the road proceeds along the north side of the Loire. (Your first view of this stately river.) There are many places where you can draw in and admire the view.

Cross the river at Les Rosiers to Gennes and continue along the south bank (D751) towards Saumur. You will drive through some delightful little villages nestling against the hillside, and there are many areas designated for picnics. In the spring the verges are covered with cowslips.

St Hilaire-St Florent

4km before Saumur, you will come to St Hilaire-St Florent, where there is the 'Musée du Champignons' with an exhibition of old tools and materials used in mushroom production. This is well worth stopping at (closed at lunchtime). Here mushrooms are cultivated in caves and they also sell local wines and cheeses.

Saumur

Continue to Saumur, passing the École de Cavalerie as you enter the town.

The École de Cavalerie is situated in the Avenue Maréchal-Foch. There has been a Cavalry School here since 1763, it has been the headquarters for the most prestigious of regiments, such as the famous 'Carabiniers de Monsieur' (i.e. the Duke of Orléans). This establishment later became known as the Cadre Noir because of its well-known black uniform. The Cadre Noir ceased to be part of the army in 1969, but it still exists as the elite of the nearby riding school.

The Cavalry School no longer exists, it is now the National School of Equitation, and it is the premier riding school in France. Every year at the end of July the famous 'Carrousel' is held in Saumur. This is a military tattoo and lasts for about four days. The army carry out manoeuvres with helicopters and tanks from the School of the Armoured Corps, who are still at the old École de Cavalerie. There are also displays of horsemanship by the Cadre Noir.

Arrangements can be made to visit the National School of Equitation by prior appointment. Details can be obtained from the Saumur Tourist Office.

Lunch at Saumur

Saumur was once a very prosperous port mainly because of the wine production in the area. It is an extremely elegant town and one of the most pleasant on the Loire. It was a very popular centre for British tourists in the Victorian and Edwardian eras. There is very little industry in Saumur because of its close proximity to Tours and Angers which are the area's centres of heavy industry. The town is dominated by the château.

The château was built in the 14th century by Louis, Duc d'Anjou who was the brother of Charles V. In the 18th century the north-west side of the château was demolished to give a better view of the Loire. It really is a most fantastic view. Under Napoleon it was a prison and eventually in 1908 the town of Saumur acquired it and restored the château to its original beauty. René of Anjou, the Poet King, referred to Saumur as 'The Castle of Love'. It is a particularly beautiful château. A contemporary illustration can be seen in miniature in the *Très Riches Heures du Duc de Berry*, where it looks far more ornate than it does today.

The Musée du Cheval is housed here, this museum depicts the horse throughout history. There is also the Musée d'Arts Decoratifs which is an interesting museum specialising in antique furniture, tapestries and porcelain. It is well worth a visit just to see the wonderful collection of 13th-century enamel crucifixes from Limoges.

The château is open daily from July 1st to September 30th from 9am until 6.30pm. During the months of July and August it is open in the evenings 8.30pm until 10.30pm. April 1st until June 30th and the month of October it is open from 9am until 11.30am and 2pm until 6.0pm. The month of November to the end of March it is open each day except Tuesday 9.30am until 11.30am and 2pm until 5pm.

Leave Saumur on the D947 to Montsoreau, with its imposing 15th-century château, where the rivers Loire and Vienne meet, and where you leave Anjou for Touraine. Take the D7 as far as the Centrale Nucléaire, following the valley along a very pretty road through fields and woodland. Follow the D749 through Avoine and Beaumont-en-Véron to Chinon.

Chinon

When you reach Chinon, cross the bridge, turn right and follow the Vienne river until you come to the Place Jeanne d'Arc where there is a large equestrian statue of the Maid of Orléans.

Dinner and overnight at Chinon.

L'Escargot
30 rue du Maréchal-Leclerc
Saumur
Tel: (41) 51 20 88

With a name like L'Escargot, it should be a super restaurant, which it is. It specialises in fish dishes, and the grilled Loire Salmon is delicious. What I like about this restaurant is that they have two excellent fixed menus.

Closed:	November, Tuesday evenings, Wednesdays out of season
Prices:	Reasonable
Rating:	★★★

USEFUL INFORMATION: SAUMUR

Tourist Office:	Place de la Bilange Tel: (41) 51 03 06

Hôtel Diderot
4 rue Buffon et 7 rue Diderot
37500 Chinon
Tel: (47) 93 18 87

Superbly situated close to the centre (off Place Jeanne d'Arc) but very quiet. You will be greeted by Mr Theo Kazamias the proprietor of the hotel; he has owned the hotel since 1978 and maintains high standards of comfort. Mr Kazamias speaks English very well. This is a very old hotel, beautifully furnished with antiques and it has a wonderful atmosphere created by the wooden beams and stone walls.

There are telephones in all rooms, and the hotel has some rooms designed for handicapped people. The hotel unfortunately has no restaurant but there are many in easy walking distance. Breakfast is served in the 15th-century dining room with its imposing fireplace. You must try the home-made jams made by Mrs Kazamias (see p. 153).

Mr Kazamias holds local wine-tastings in his bar, and he will arrange trips to the vineyards that abound in the area.

Open all year
Rooms: 20 (10 with bath, 10 with shower),
                    all with private WC
Facilities: Some rooms designed for the
                    handicapped, telephones in rooms,
                    no restaurant, parking (hotel
                    courtyard)
Credit cards: Visa, AmEx
Rating: ★★★

Grand Hôtel de la Boule d'Or
69 Quai Jeanne d'Arc
Chinon
Tel: (47) 93 03 13

This is an old coaching inn, but the coaching area is now the restaurant, where you dine surrounded by vines and roses. Prices — reasonable. Setting — very good (some rooms overlook the Loire).

Closed: December 15-February 1
Rating: ★★★

Restaurant le St-Maxime
31 Place de Général de Gaulle
(right at the side of the town hall)
Chinon

Do not be put off by the facade, it resembles a bar, but once inside you will find a comfortable restaurant. The owner Mr Lionel Petetgars, runs it like a ship, one lovely touch is that you receive a complimentary drink upon arrival and the food is excellent. Try the Rillettes de Saumon de Loire or Moules Normandie as a starter. Excellent wine list, specialising in the wines of the area.

Credit cards: Visa
Rating: ★★★

Au Plaisir Gourmand
2 rue Parmentier
Chinon
Tel: (47) 93 20 48

It has a small dining room in an 18th-century building and has loads of atmosphere. Try the warm oysters with leeks and the steamed chicken with truffles.

Closed: Sunday evenings and Monday
                   lunchtimes
Credit cards: none
Rating: ★★★

USEFUL INFORMATION: CHINON

Postal address:	37500 Indre-et-Loire
Population:	8,800
Altitude:	125 M
Distances:	Angers 75 km, Loches 58 km, Paris 280 km, Saumur 32 km
Tourist Office:	12 rue Voltaire Tel: (47) 93 17 85

Annual events:
Every Friday and Saturday there is a historical evening in the château from mid-June to mid-September.
July/August: dramatic and musical evenings in the town.
Towards the end of July there is an Antiques Fair.
Early August: Medieval Festivals, the whole town takes part.

The flower market, Chinon

DAY 2

Chinon, Fontevraud Abbey, La Devinière, approx. 46 km (29 miles)

You will be spending the morning in Chinon, discovering the beautiful old town and visiting the château. Try and fit all this in, and allow time for the half hour drive to Fontevraud l'Abbaye, for lunch. After lunch you will visit the abbey.

The return journey will take you via La Devinière which has associations with Rabelais. You will not have driven so far today and you should arrive back in plenty of time for dinner and relaxation.

Overnight at Chinon

Map references:
Chinon	0°14′E 47°10′N
Fontevraud l'Abbaye	0°03′E 47°11′N
La Devinière	0°10′E 47°08′N

Route shown p. 42.

Breakfast at Chinon

Chinon

After a 'jammy' breakfast, walk through the winding streets of 15th- and 18th-century turreted houses before you visit the château.

Chinon is a very wonderful small town, full of character and history. You can see the house in Rue Voltaire where it is said that Rabelais lived, Chinon claims that he was born there, but it is highly likely that he was born in the village of La Devinière not far from the town. The type of people he described so beautifully in his books can still be seen in Chinon and the surrounding countryside, you feel as though you have put the clock back.

Walk down the streets Rue J-J Rousseau and Rue Voltaire, in season flowers abound everywhere in window boxes, and on a spring or summer evening the perfume is outstanding. In these streets you will find the oldest houses in Chinon (14th- to 16th-century) and do not be startled if you see an old lady who strongly resembles the mother of Rembrandt, Chinon breeds characters like that. Now to the château.

The château consists actually of three castles, standing majestically over the town. Unfortunately most is in ruins. Despite this it is well worth a visit. You will step right back to the Middle Ages.

You pass first the castle of St Georges. Henry II built this castle and actually died here in 1189, and then proceed through to the middle castle, the Château de Milieu, on the site of a Roman camp. This is entered through the *Clock Pavilion* where the Museum of Joan of Arc is situated. It dates from the 11th to 15th century. You then walk through to the third castle, and come to the remains of the Great Hall, where Joan of Arc first met the Dauphin, and announced, 'Gentle Dauphin, I am called Jeanne the Maid, and the King of Heaven sends to you His commandment by me, that you are to be crowned at Reims and that you are to be lieutenant of the King of Heaven, as the King of France rightly is'. She asked at once that the court should support her in what she had to do, that being to raise the siege of Orléans.

During her stay in Chinon, Joan of Arc lived in the Coudray Tower, in the third castle, which is very well preserved.

The château is open every day except Wednesday, 9am-noon and 2pm-6pm. It closes at 5pm in the winter and is closed during the months of January and February. In the summer there are Son-et-Lumière performances.

There are plenty of interesting tours and excursions you can join in Chinon. You may wish to take an evening cruise on the 'Bâteau Mouche' which leaves from the camping site in Chinon. The cruise is on the Vienne and the Loire and goes as far as Montsoreau. On board you can have dinner and there is dancing. It is essential that you book and this can be done by telephoning (47) 93 08 35. The tourist office organises tours around the old part of the town during the season and you can also book boat trips on the river Vienne. What about a train trip on the famous Touraine Steam Train which runs from Chinon to Richelieu? It operates from mid-May to mid-September, for further details telephone (47) 58 36 29.

Leave Chinon on the D749 to St Lazare. Turn right onto the D751, left by Candes-St Martin and left onto the D947.

Fontevraud l'Abbaye

Lunch at Fontevraud l'Abbaye

The Abbey was founded in 1099 by Robert d'Arbissel. The 12th-century church has four Byzantine domes. But apart from the architectural interest, if you are British you really have to visit the Abbey, for this is where the tomb of Richard the Lion Heart is situated, as well as those of Henry II, Eleanor of Guienne, and Queen Isabella of Angoulême. It is possible that the effigies are near where they were actually buried, as the graves were found near a pillar of the main tower, the Tour d'Evraud.

In 1867 Napoleon III offered to return the tombs of the Kings to England at the request of Queen Victoria. There was such a public outcry in France, he had to write to the Queen asking to be relieved of the offer.

The Abbey is in the course of reconstruction, but do not be put off by this, as it has been going on for many years. The Abbey must have been a little city on its own, and it was for both men and women. This was very unusual in the 12th century, both the monks and nuns were under the direction of an Abbess, who was often a royal princess, so only nuns from wealthy families went there.

The Abbey has the last remaining Romanesque kitchen in France. There are some very interesting frescoes in the chapterhouse. The cloister dates from the same period and the refectory is from the 16th century. See also the gardens, ponds and the orangery.

Fontevraud l'Abbaye is open from 9am-noon and 2pm-6.30pm all the year with the exception of the beginning of April to the end of September when it is 9am-noon and 2pm-4pm.

La Devinière

Leave the village and continue on D947 which becomes D147 as far as Roiffé. Turn left onto D48 through Chavigny to La Devinière.

Here you will find the home of the father of Rabelais (Antoine Rabelais), who was a lawyer at the court of Chinon. It is certain that the young François Rabelais used to visit this house. Every room of the house and even the dovecot, houses exhibits which together form the museum of Rabelais, as well as a good collection of local furniture of the 16th and 17th century. This is altogether a fascinating museum. Leave La Devinière and continue out on the D759, turn right at the crossroads onto the D749, turn left at St Lazare to Chinon.

Dinner and overnight at Chinon.

Hôtel La Croix Blanche
Fontevraud l'Abbaye
49590 Maine-et-Loire
Tel: (41) 51 71 11

You will find this good hotel right opposite the entrance to the Abbey. Here you can obtain an excellent lunch at reasonable prices, the menu specialises in regional cooking. The hotel has recently been renovated, it has a lovely dining room, but you can also choose to have a simple omelette and salad in the bar. The rooms are all well-appointed. The hotel is owned by Mme Thairery.

Rooms:	22
Credit cards:	Not accepted
Rating:	★★

USEFUL INFORMATION: FONTEVRAUD L'ABBAYE

Postal Address:	49590 Maine-et-Loire
Population:	1,850
Distances:	Paris 294km, Angers 69km, Chinon 21km, Saumur 16km
Tourist Office:	à la Mairie
	Tel: (41) 51 71 21

Azay-le-Rideau

DAY 3

Chinon, Ussé, Villandry, Savonnières, Azay-le-Rideau: approx. 64 km (40 miles)

Set out straight after breakfast, as you have a very full day ahead of you. First to the elegant château of Ussé, then crossing the Loire to visit the château of Langeais.

After lunch at Villandry, a stroll through the fascinating gardens of the château is followed by an adventure underground in the Grottos of Savonnières where the temperature is only 14°C (so do have some warm clothing available).

At the end of this long but very interesting day, you will be thankful for the comfort of your hotel in Azay-le-Rideau.

Overnight at Azay-le-Rideau

Map references:
Chinon	0°14'E 47°10'N
Ussé	0°18'E 47°15'N
Langeais	0°24'E 47°20'N
Villandry	0°31'E 47°20'N
Savonnières	0°33'E 47°21'N
Azay-le-Rideau	0°28'E 47°16'N

Route shown p. 74.

Breakfast at Chinon

Leave Chinon on the D16 through Huismes. Turn right on the D7 to Ussé.

Ussé

The tiny village is dominated by its château, sometimes called château de la Belle au Bois Dormant, or the castle of the Sleeping Beauty, for this was the inspiration for Perrault's fairy tale. The interior of the château can be visited only when escorted by a French speaking guide. However you can visit the gardens, Chapel and Sleeping Beauty Tower on your own, which I advise, for the château's greatest beauty is its exterior.

This very splendid château is situated on the edge of the forest of Chinon. It was built on the foundations of an ancient fortress in the 16th and 17th centuries by the Bueil and d'Espinay families. Visit the chapel and see its sculptured porches and stalls built by Charles d'Espinay in 1538, and wander through the gardens and terraces full of orange trees. The royal apartments were designed by Mlle D'Ussé for the anticipated visit of Louis XIV. The visit never took place. The property is privately owned by the descendants of the Count of Blacas. The château is very imposing from whatever angle one views it.

There are helicopter flights from Ussé around the châteaux of this area of the Loire — Blois, Azay-le-Rideau, Amboise and Chenonceaux. The château is open from Easter until the end of September, 9am-noon, 2pm-7pm. It closes an hour earlier in October and November.

Leave Ussé and continue on the D7 as far as Lignières-de-Touraine, then turn left on the D57 and cross the Loire to Langeais.

Langeais

As you drive into the small town you will see the château standing above the centre of Langeais. The first impression is one of a rather depressing fortress building — compared to the elegant exterior of Ussé.

The château dates back to the ninth century when the dreaded Black Falcon built what is considered to be the first dungeon in France, you can see the ruins to this day. The original château was captured by the English in 1427 and it was sold to the French on the condition that it was pulled down. The keep, which is one of the oldest towers in France and is 10th-century, is all that remains of the old château. The present château was built in the reign of Louis XI in 1465.

The interior of the château is very well preserved, it took a period of 18 years to renovate it. The work was carried out by Jacques Siegried the well-known theatrical producer of the time who bought it in 1886 and bequeathed it to the Institute of France in 1904.

The marriage of the fourteen-year-old Anne of Brittany to the twenty-one-year-old Charles VIII took place here in a large room on the first floor. This marriage brought about the unification of France and Brittany. In the guard room you will see their symbols: fleurs-de-lis, scallops and ermine. There are seven tapestries in the wedding chamber which decorate the walls and these are known as the 'Valiant Knights'. The gardens are also well worth a visit.

The château is open from mid-March to mid-September, 9am-12 noon, 2pm-6.30pm.

Whilst you are in the town of Langeais you may wish to visit the house where it is said that Rabelais lived for a time, this is a Renaissance house and is in the square directly opposite the château. If you go into the Rue Anne-de-Bretagne you will see two excellent examples of 16th-century houses.

Return to Lignières-de-Touraine and continue on the D7 to Villandry for lunch.

Villandry

Villandry is the last of the Renaissance châteaux to be built on the Loire. Jean le Breton (who originally came from Scotland) was finance minister to François I, and he built Villandry between 1532 and 1536, on what is believed to be the foundations of an ancient fortress.

The château of Villandry is beautifully proportioned. The appearance is very much a French interpretation of Italian renaissance style. It has arcaded galleries, richly decorated windows with pilasters and sculptured gables, backed by high and steeply sloping slate roofs. Part of the interior is open to the public from Easter to the end of October — whereas the gardens are open from 9am until dusk throughout the year. The tour of the château includes the salons, the dining room and the main staircase. There are many Spanish paintings and much beautiful furniture to admire. You can then go up to the terraces, which overlook the valley on one side and the gardens on the other.

Jean le Breton designed the gardens. He was later involved in the building of Chambord (see p. 102). He had been Ambassador to Italy, and there he studied the art of planning gardens with special emphasis on the 'Italian Renaissance Garden'. Hence the gardens of Villandry, which should take pride of place in any visit to the château for they are, in my estimation, some of the finest in the Loire valley. There are several gardens each with its own distinct character.

The tiers of gardens begin with the highest being the water garden, with its fine expanse of water, below this is the ornamental garden, with its geometrically shaped flower beds, with box borders and shaped yew trees. Below this in the most important position is the kitchen garden. So many new vegetables were being brought from America, this garden was of special interest and was overlooked by the château.

Each ornamental garden tells a story:

1) *L'Amour Tragique* — boxwoods are pruned in the shape of swords and daggers, and red flowers denote the blood which has been split in the cause of women.

2) *L'Amour Adultéré* — symbolised by fan-shaped hedge borders depicting flirtation. The flowers are all yellow, the colour symbolic of betrayed love.

3) *L'Amour Tendre* — this garden is designed with hearts and the flowers are orange, conveying flames of love.

4) *L'Amour Passioné* — once again the motif is hearts, but this time they are shattered by passion.

5) *The Kitchen Garden* — the garden is split into nine equal squares divided by wide walkways. On every corner there is a bower covered with roses and jasmine, where you can sit in the shade. In the centre of each square there is a small fountain for watering purposes. Every square is divided into different geometrical patterns by dwarf box hedges, and filled with a variety of vegetables of different colours to complete the pattern. The squares are outlined with a border of flowers and small cordoned fruit trees.

6) *The Herb Garden* — this lies between the kitchen garden and the village. It is a smaller less formal garden of rectangular beds packed with at least thirty varieties of herbs with aromatic, flavouring and medicinal properties.

The gardens are now privately owned by M. Carvallo who lives in the château. They are open 9am to sunset. You can visit the château with a guide, 9am-6.30pm.

Leave Villandry and continue on the D7 to Savonnières.

Savonnières

The Grottos of Savonnières are close by, and are well worth visiting. There are two grottos, the first one was discovered in 1547, this is full of stalactites, a lake, underground passages, a Gallo-Roman cemetery, and there is a terrific reconstruction of prehistoric fauna. The second grotto was only discovered in 1947. Wrap up well, the temperature in the Grottos is only 14°C.

Open: February 8-March 31, 9am-noon, 2pm-6.30pm; April 1-October 15, 9am-6pm; October 16-December 20, 9am-noon, 2pm-6pm.

Leave the Grottos and return to Villandry. Turn left onto the D121 through Druye, and then turn right onto the D751 to Azay-le-Rideau, where you will stay for two nights.

Dinner and overnight at Azay-le-Rideau.

Le Cheval Rouge
Villandry
Tel: (47) 50 02 07

Close to the château, this restaurant specialises in fish dishes and game. Prices are moderate for a fixed meal, but à la carte can be expensive.

Closed: November-March, Mondays in April, May, September and October

Rating: ★★★

USEFUL INFORMATION: VILLANDRY

Postal Address: 37 Indre-et-Loire
Population: 742
Distances: Paris 252km, Azay-le-Rideau 10km, Saumur 52km

Hôtel du Grand Monarque
Place République
37190 Azay-le-Rideau
Tel: (44) 45 40 08

This is a most comfortable and friendly hotel, with good value prices. The owner is John-Michel Forest, who was a well known French sports journalist. He acquired the hotel in 1988 from the famous Jacquet family who bought the hotel in 1900 and it remained in the family until 1988. It is 200 years old and has a wonderful atmosphere. Ask to see the real live 'wild' boar, whose name is Eglantine. She lives at the back of the hotel.

There is an excellent menu and the chef is Alain Brisacier who joined the hotel in 1977. He specialises in many local dishes. The hotel has a very impressive wine cellar, with many varieties of local wines as well as Chinon.

The Maître d'Hôtel is Daniel Franchineau, who is always on hand to help and guide you in the selection of your wines.

Many well-known personalities have either stayed or dined at the hotel over the years. These have included the Duke and Duchess of Windsor, the Queen Mother, and President Truman.

Rooms:	28
Facilities:	Restaurant
Credit cards:	Visa, AmEx, Mastercard
Rating:	★★★★

Hotel Balzac
rue A-Riché
Azay-le-Rideau
Tel: (47) 45 42 08

Open all year
Rooms:	12
Facilities:	Parking
Credit cards:	Eurocard, Visa
Rating:	★★

USEFUL INFORMATION: AZAY-LE-RIDEAU

Postal Address:	37190 Indre-et-Loire
Population:	3,000
Altitude:	50M
Distances:	Paris 255 km, Chinon 25km, Saumur 46 km
Tourist Office:	Rue Gambetta (Town Hall out of season) Tel: (47) 45 42 11

Troglodyte house in Villaines-les-Rochers

DAY 4

Azay-le-Rideau, Villaines-les-Rochers, Saché, Azay-le-Rideau: approx. 20 km
(12 miles)

A leisurely morning is spent exploring Azay-le-Rideau and the château,
followed by a light lunch in the centre of town. In the afternoon I suggest a
short drive along quiet roads to Villaines-les-Rochers. A unique village noted for
its willow baskets and troglodyte dwellings. Continuing on this circular tour,
you will visit Saché, where Balzac lived, returning to Azay-le-Rideau in plenty of
time for an aperitif, before another succulent dinner.

Overnight at Azay-le-Rideau

Map references:
Azay-le-Rideau   0°28′E 47°16′N
Villaines-les-Rochers   0°30′E 47°14′N
Saché   0°33′E 47°15′N

Route shown p. 74.

Breakfast at Azay-le-Rideau

The morning's exploration of Azay-le-Rideau begins with a visit to the château.

This is considered to be the second most popular château in the Touraine region (Chinon is the most popular). The river Indre flows on two sides. I love to see it floodlit at night from the outside. Visit it during the morning but return again at night. During the summer there are performances of 'Son-et-Lumière'.

The château has quite a history. It was first a private house during the Renaissance. In 1418 it was a fortress held by a Burgundian garrison. When Charles VII was Dauphin, he was insulted by the Burgundian soldiery as he passed through the region. He was so incensed, that the men were executed and the building was burnt to the ground. For many years after that the village was known as Azay-le-Brulé (Azay-the-burnt). Eventually it reverted to its original name, taken from its founder Ridel, Lord of Azay.

A century after the burning in 1518, Gilles Berthelot the royal financier began the new building on the same site. The château was built on piles driven into the river bed rather like Chenonceaux (see p. 76). The proportions of the château are superb, with its slim towers and unified design. You will be enchanted by its graceful lines reflecting the influence of Gille's wife Philippe Lesbahy. The setting enhances its attraction, the expanse of water, the English-style park and the great avenues of trees. The Gothic features such as the machicolations are fake. They are there to enrich the decorative appearance. Berthelot did not have much time to enjoy his château, François I grew jealous and he had to flee and died in exile.

Visit the Banqueting Hall, which includes some very fine tapestries showing scenes from the life of Constantine, and a complete kitchen from former times. In the ground floor bedroom, there is an excellent example of a 16th-century four poster bed.

Look out over the grounds from the Royal Chamber, from this viewpoint, I am sure you will agree they present an impressive spectacle. As you enter the château you will see the salamander of François I, a symbol which will be seen again in many of the châteaux of the Loire.

The château is open eve⌐ ,
out of season). There are cυ.
speaking guides.

Lunch at Azay-le-Rideau

Have a light lunch at the Renaissance Salon de Thé. This is situated in the centre of the town. Whilst you dine notice the willow furniture which is made in the village you will be visiting in the afternoon.

Leave Azay-le-Rideau on the D17/57 through La Vallée to Villaines-les-Rochers.

Villaines-les-Rochers

Here you will enter a wonderworld of fascinating troglodyte houses in caves carved out of the hillsides.

This is a centre of the ancient craft of basket-making. If you take the backroads of the village you will be intrigued by seeing the profusion of willows. You are surrounded by all stages of the craft. Bleached and skinned, willows lie in stooks outside the houses, and everywhere you will see them on drying racks. You can watch them being made into everything from bird-cages to furniture of all types, shapes and sizes. The work of the village is sent to major outlets in France and exported all over the world. It is wonderful to see the art of basket-making being carried out exactly as it has been for centuries. Time seems to have stood still, although I must say life years ago must have been extremely hard for the basket-maker, earning a living from his art with very little reward.

It all started many years ago when the local gentry and nobility were traditionally presented with basket cages full of birds, mainly pigeons, which on the feast of Pentecost, were released from the top of cathedrals and main churches to represent the Holy Ghost.

'La Corporation des Vanniers et Quincailliers de Paris' was formed in 1467, and in 1849 the 'Société des Vanniers de Villaines' was formed and is today one of France's oldest Guilds.

Touraine is proud of its basket-making industry, and there is even a song which is sung throughout the area at all major fêtes called 'La Chanson du Vannier' (The Basketweaver's Song). You can buy the goods that are made in the village at several shops and showrooms, it may appear to you that they are a little expensive, but they will last and the design and craftsmanship are excellent.

Observing my wife sketching in this unusual village and seeing an old wine press by the roadside, the rock dwellings, and patches of willow growing by the streams I very quickly realised that this is an artist's paradise. As we drove past the homes and farms of these true country people, they waved greetings, and we were struck by their personalities, their faces are a bonus to the artist and the photographer. I would be surprised if you did not hear somebody whistling or humming a little of 'La Chanson du Vannier' as you passed by.

Continue through the village onto an un-numbered road signposted Saché.

Saché

You will drive through neatly cordoned apple orchards and when you arrive in Saché, head straight for the car park in the centre of the village. Here you will see a 'Mobile Statue' presented to the village by Alexander Calder in 1974.

Saché is a beautiful and tranquil village, and often missed by English visitors who are possibly concentrating too much on the châteaux as they are passing through and missing the other delights of the Loire valley. You will find Saché very relaxing. Walk from the car park and turn right and you will arrive at the small 17th-century château where Balzac (1799-1850) wrote *Le Lys dans la Vallée, La Recherche de l'Absolu, Louis Lambert* and *Père Goriot*. You can wander around the grounds, which are very romantic, and stand in the gardens and watch the swallows in the early evening sun — certainly a picture of pure beauty. Honoré de Balzac has often been compared to Charles Dickens, and the years that he spent in Saché are considered to have been the literary peak of his life. You can visit the interior of the château, where there is an exhibition.

The château is open: March 15-September 30, 9am-noon and 2pm-6pm; October 1-March 14, 9am-noon, 2pm-5pm. Closed on Wednesdays.

Before leaving, visit the 12th-century village church beside the car park. Leave Saché turning left onto the D17 and back to Azay-le-Rideau.

Dinner and overnight at Azay-le-Rideau.

A sixteenth-century house, Sancerre

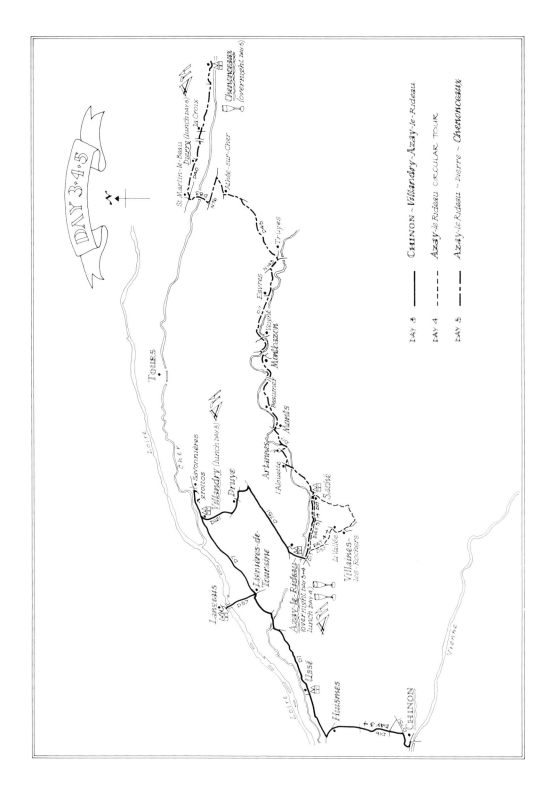

DAY 3·4·5

TOURS

Loire

Cher

Loire

Vienne

St-Martin-le-Beau
Dierre (lunch Day 5)
la Croix
Athée-sur-Cher
D40
D83
N76
D45
Truyes
N143
Esvres
D17
Veigné
Montbazon
Savonnières
Ballan
Villandry (lunch Day 3)
Druye
Artannes
Monts
l'Alouette
Saché
la Vallée
Villaines-les-Rochers
Lignières-de-Touraine
Villandry
D121
D7
D57
Langeais
Ussé
Huismes
CHINON
Azay-le-Rideau (overnight Day 3 & 4) (lunch Day 4)
Chenonceaux (overnight Day 5)
D57
D1
D16
Day 3 & 4
Day 5

CHINON ~ Villandry ~ Azay-le-Rideau

Azay-le-Rideau CIRCULAR TOUR

Azay-le-Rideau ~ Dierre ~ Chenonceaux

DAY 3 ————————

DAY 4 – – – – – –

DAY 5 –·–·–·–·

DAY 5

Azay-le-Rideau, Dierre, Chenonceaux approx. 60 km (40 miles)

I am sure you would like to linger longer, but ahead of you there is a long morning's drive. This is not one of the most interesting routes on your tour, but it is direct, and the destination is in itself a splendid reward for your perseverance.

Lunch at the 'Auberge des Ailes' in Dierre, before spending the whole of the afternoon at the château of Chenonceaux and its gardens. Refreshments are available in the Orangery, if you prefer a light lunch there.

Both the recommended hotels are in Chenonceaux, so you have only a short drive down the road at the end of the day.

Overnight at Chenonceaux.

Map references:
Azay-le-Rideau	0°28′E 47°16′N
Dierre	0°58′E 47°21′N
Chenonceaux	1°04′E 47°20′N

Breakfast at Azay-le-Rideau.

Leave Azay-le-Rideau on the D17. Follow the country road through Saché, l'Alouette and Monts to Beaumer. The road then passes through a more or less continuously built-up area through Montbazon, Veigné and Esvres to Truyes. Turn left onto the D45, through Athée onto the N76 westwards. Turn right onto the D83 and cross the river Cher to St Martin-le-Beau. Then follow the D40 as far as Dierre.

Dierre

This is a very good place to stop for an early lunch and there is an excellent little auberge called Auberge des Ailes.

Continue on the D40 through La Croix along the north bank of the river Cher until you arrive in Chenonceaux.

Chenonceaux

This is one of the most elegant châteaux in the whole of France. Make a point of arriving as early in the afternoon as you can because tourists from all over the world visit to admire its wonderful architectural beauty, so it is often crowded. However, if you do not visit Chenonceaux, you will miss a major highlight in any tour of the Loire.

You approach the château down an avenue of plane trees, as you walk you will feel a tingle of sheer excitement as it unfolds before you. You cross the drawbridge and there it stands in all its majesty. Look up at the turrets and the window frames which are so richly decorated. Walk through the great chamber which rests on the arches over the river. Keep your camera loaded and at the ready, at every turning you will find something of interest to record for posterity. As you stand and look out over the grounds at the cedar trees and giant oaks, you will feel that you are at the centre of French history.

Women have certainly been to the forefront of the history at Chenonceaux. The first was Catherine Briconnet who was the wife of Thomas Bohier who laid the foundations in 1513. Immediately after the death of Thomas Bohier she carried on with the work of creating Chenonceaux. Then came Henry II who gave it as a gift to his mistress, the famous beauty, Diane de Poitiers. When he died his wife, Catherine de Medici (whom you will meet again at Blois), banished Diane to

Chaumont (p. 93), and took Chenonceaux for herself, where she entertained in lavish style. She built the long gallery over the bridge, and organised sumptuous feasts and festivals. Young women, dressed as mermaids, welcomed guests from the moats, nymphs sang in the woodland. Catherine had a celebrated flying troupe of young beauties which she used to seduce both friend and foe. She planned an extravagant ball for her favourite son, Henry III. Honoré de Balzac wrote in *Le Lys dans la Vallée* the following lurid description of a fête at Chenonceaux.

> The author of *Castles of the Loire in the Renaissance Period* (Hachette, La vie quotidienne), Ivan Cloulas, vividly recalls the parties and festivals that took place there. He comments at length upon a ball given by Catherine de Medici, in honour of Henri III and his companions in the gardens of Chenonceaux:
>
> 'The king arrived, as it was his custom for masked balls, dressed as a woman. His doublet was cut very low to show off his chest and he wore a string of pearls and three collars, two ruffled and one turned down, exactly as was then fashionable among the ladies of the court.
>
> Witticisms about the woman-king and man-queen were exchanged as the king sat surrounded by his minions. They too were all made up, with their hair dyed and curled, perfumed and wearing large heavy ruffs. They were served by the younger women of the court, half-naked and their hair loose and dishevelled. They wore scanty male costumes in two-coloured damask.
>
> One of the hostesses was Madame de Sauvre, afterwards the Marquise of Noirmoutiers, a beautiful and spirited woman who went from man to man as she pleased. Other beauties present were Madame de Guercheville, nicknamed 'La Jeune' and the devilish Chateauneuf who only a few days later stabbed her unfaithful husband to death. These were the main guests at this monstrous gathering where only the most pagan of virtues were evident.'

The manners and morals of Chenonceaux changed when the widow of Henry III, Louise de Vaudemont, inherited the château. She was known as the white queen, because she always wore white, the colour worn by mourning queens. She lived in seclusion and made no additions to the structure. Thereafter it passed from hand to hand.

The last lady of Chenonceaux was the wife of General Dupain, who bought it from the Duke of Bourbon. The château escaped damage during the

Revolution, thanks to the popularity of Madame Dupain, who was loved and respected by everyone in the region. Chenonceaux was designed by women so hence they are known as the ladies of Chenonceaux and their tale is told today in music and song.

As you wander around the château look at the painted ceiling in the Salle des Gardes and the door carved with panels dedicated to Saints Thomas and Catherine who were the patron saints of the Bohier family. Walk through to the Chambre de Diane de Poitiers and the Cabinet Vert, both furnished in the style of Catherine de Medici. In the Chambre de François I you will see letters signed by Diane de Poitiers while in the Grand Salon hang paintings by Canaletto and Rubens.

Chenonceaux, during the early part of the 1939-45 war, lay half in unoccupied France and the other in occupied France; the dividing line was the Grand Salon over the river.

Visit the gardens which are a sheer delight, and you can hire a rowing boat on the river Cher, what a wonderful way to spend a sunny summer afternoon. The largest garden in front of the château was designed by Diane de Poitiers and the one towards the back was designed by Catherine de Medici. Both in the Renaissance style, paths, hedges, small trees and formal flower beds.

You can learn more of the details of the history of Chenonceaux by visiting the Wax Museum (well-signposted) which is excellently presented. There is a Son-et-Lumière during the summer months called 'In the olden days of the women of Chenonceaux'. If you chose not to have an early lunch at Dierre, there is a self-service restaurant in the château grounds.

The château is open: mid-March-mid-September, 9am-7pm; mid-September-31 October, 9am-6pm; November, 9am-5pm; December-January 9am-noon, 2pm-4pm; February-mid-March, 9am-noon, 2pm-5pm.

Dinner and overnight at Chenonceaux.

Hôtel du Bon-Labourer et du Château
Chenonceaux
37150 Bléré
Tel: (47) 29 90 02

This is one of the finest hotels in the Loire valley, and is acclaimed by most of the well known food writers as being the height of French cuisine. It is not cheap, but not maddeningly expensive. The food is out of this world and the hotel was founded in 1880. Part of the building goes back to 1880 but obviously there have been additions over the years. It is run by Louis-Claude Jeudi (what a glorious name, Mr Thursday!) and his wife.

Closed:	December-February
Rooms:	29
Credit cards:	most major cards — AmEx, Visa, Diners, etc.
Rating:	★★★★

It is essential that you book early, preferably before you leave on your holiday, as this hotel is extremely popular.

Hôtel Renaudière
Chenonceaux
37150 Bléré
Tel: (47) 23 90 04

A good family hotel. Once again, in the peak season book before you leave on your holiday. The prices are very reasonable.

Closed:	November 16-February inclusive
Rooms:	12
Facilities:	Restaurant
Credit cards:	Visa
Rating:	★★

Auberge des Ailes
Dierre
Tel: (47) 57 93 84

It is not very impressive from the outside, but it has excellent food and at very reasonable prices. This is a family restaurant, and we have eaten here several times in the past and have always gone away completely satisfied. You can park opposite the Auberge, but be careful as it is a very busy main road.

Closed: Tuesdays
Rating: ★

Au Gâteau Breton
Chenonceaux
Tel: (47) 29 90 14

This is a very good restaurant in the centre of the village. The prices are moderate, the food is excellent.

Closed: Mid-November-mid-December,
                           Tuesdays
Rating: ★★★

USEFUL INFORMATION: CHENONCEAUX

Postal Address: 37 Indre-et-Loire
Population: 361
Distances: Paris 234km, Amboise 12km
Tourist Office: rue Château
                     Tel: (47) 23 94 45

Chenonceaux from a drawbridge

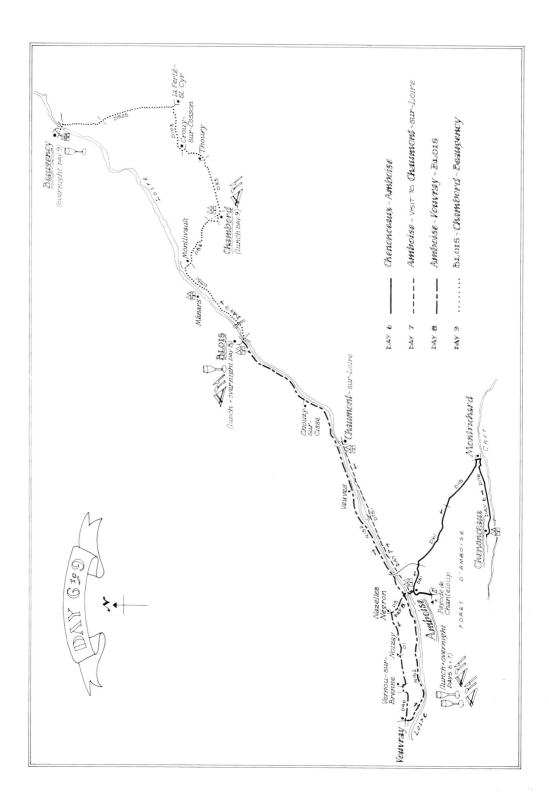

DAY 6 to 9

Chenonceaux–Amboise ── DAY 6

Amboise – visit to Chaumont–sur–Loire ─ ─ ─ DAY 7

Amboise–Vouvray–Blois ─ · ─ DAY 8

Blois–Chambord–Beaugency · · · · · · · DAY 9

Beaugency (overnight day 9)

la Ferté-St Cyr

Crouy-sur-Cosson

Thoury

Chambord (lunch day 9)

Montlivault

Ménars

BLOIS (lunch – overnight day 8)

Chouzy-sur-Cisse

Chaumont-sur-Loire

Veuves

Montrichard

Chenonceaux DAY 6

FORÊT D'AMBOISE

Pagode de Chanteloup

Nazelles Negron

Amboise (lunch-overnight Days 6-7)

Vernou-sur-Brenne

Vouzay

Vouvray

Loire

Loire

Cher

D925

D103

D33

D84

D960

RN 152

D1

D46

RN152

D62

RN152

D31

D40

D115

D62

D176

D115

DAY 6

Chenonceaux, Montrichard, Amboise: approx. 33 km (21 miles)

After breakfast, you have a short but interesting drive to Amboise, through Montrichard. After lunch in Amboise, at a restaurant of your choice, the afternoon will be spent discovering the delights of this town, which will include patisserie specialities, and a short walk to Clos-Lucé, the home of Leonardo da Vinci for the last four years of his life. The walk back down the hill will take you past the château and on to your hotel between the château and the riverside.

Overnight at Amboise.

Map references:
Chenonceaux   1°04′E 47°20′N
Montrichard   1°11′E 47°21′N
Amboise   1°00′E 47°25′N

Breakfast at Chenonceaux.

Leave Chenonceaux on the D176 to Montrichard.

Montrichard

Montrichard has a large 11th-century keep that rises majestically above the town. Here, in the centre of Touraine wines, you will again find troglodyte houses and caves, used not only for storing wine but also for cultivating mushrooms. The town has many 15th- and 16th-century houses and the parish church dates from the 12th century. It is altogether a beautiful place to wander in.

Take the D115 which becomes the D61 to Amboise, where you return to the banks of the Loire.

Amboise

As you drive into the town centre of Amboise, the tree-lined road takes you along the side of the Loire, you will pass the fanciful fountain decorated by Max Ernst (1891-1976), the great Surrealist painter. The Mayor of Amboise commissioned him to redesign the town's fountain — the result is amusing. There are several excellent little restaurants in the town centre for lunch.

Lunch at Amboise.

During the afternoon wander around the town of Amboise. When you reach the centre — the Place du Château — do visit Bigot's, the delightful patisserie.

Walk up the hill at the side of the château to Clos-Lucé (well-signposted). Your visit to Amboise would not be complete without seeing the house where Leonardo da Vinci lived during his years at Amboise. This 15th-century manor house is beautifully preserved and in the cellars below there is a wonderful exhibition of a collection of models (reconstructed from his drawings thanks to the multinational I.B.M.) of the inventions of the great man. It is an opportunity to really appreciate the innovative genius of Leonardo da Vinci. You will see the helicopter, the parachute, the very first aeroplane, a machine gun and much more. It is hard to believe that he envisaged these early in the 16th century. Reproductions of his sketches are here too, with his descriptions in mirror-reversed script. He was left-handed and could write backwards. It has been suggested that this was a code. Within the house, you can visit Leonardo's bedroom, the kitchen with its superb fireplace, and the Renaissance rooms. Leonardo lived here for the last four years of his life, and it is said that he died in the house in the arms of François I, on May 2, 1519.

At Clos-Lucé there is a lovely Renaissance rose garden, and do not leave before you have visited the chapel, an absolute gem in every way. This was built by Charles VIII for his queen, Anne of Britanny. In the grounds there is a coffee shop, where they serve light meals, and next door there is a video theatre showing films of the life of Leonardo.

Open daily 9am-noon, 2pm-7pm, tel: (47) 57 62 88.

For a short but interesting trip head south from Amboise through the forest of Amboise in which the Valois kings used to hunt. In about 9 km (6 miles) you will find the Pagoda de Chanteloup off the D31. This folly is all that is left of the Duc de Choiseul's château. He visited England and was so impressed by the Chinese pagoda at Kew, he built one of his own.

Return to Amboise.

On your way back to your hotel, you may wish to stop for some liquid refreshment at one of the numerous cafés around the main square.

Dinner and overnight at Amboise.

Bigot's (Salon de Thé)
Place du Château
Amboise
Tel: (47) 57 04 46

I first visited this pâtisserie in late winter, there was a lovely log fire burning, excellent real tea and scrumptious cakes. I had the pleasure of meeting four generations of the Bigot family who were having tea in the corner of the salon. Grandmother, her daughter Renée, the daughter of Renée, Christiane and her little baby. The Salon de Thé was founded in 1913. You can buy every conceivable type of gateaux and do not leave without buying some of their handmade chocolates. Christiane speaks English very well, and is available to help you in your selection. It was here that I was asked to sign her 'Gold Book', nothing could have given me more pleasure, as I would never pass within 100km of Amboise without visiting Bigot's.

Open:	Winter 8am-8pm (closed Tuesdays).
	Summer 8am-10pm.

Hôtel du Lion d'Or
17 Quai Charles Guinot
37400 Amboise
Tel: (47) 57 00 23

This is a very comfortable hotel owned by M and Mme J.M. Willieme. The food is excellent and they specialise in the dishes of the region. There is a first class wine cellar. The hotel is situated opposite the river Loire. When booking try and obtain a room at the rear of the hotel as this is quieter, and you overlook the château. The dining room is beautiful in itself, and you can have a very relaxing meal in wonderful surroundings, the main feature is the fireplace.

Closed:	November to March
Rooms:	23 (19 with private bathrooms)
Facilities:	Restaurant, parking
Credit cards:	Visa, Mastercard, Euro
Rating:	★★★

Hôtel Belle-Vue
12 Quai Charles-Guinot
37400 Amboise
Tel: (47) 57 02 26

From the outside it is not as impressive as the Hôtel du Lion d'Or, which is incidentally only two doors away, but it is very comfortable and there is a garden and swimming pool, very tastefully laid out. The restaurant, which offers a lovely riverside view, has a set menu on weekdays.

Closed:	mid-November-mid-December, January
Credit cards:	Visa
Rating:	★★★

Do you wish to live in a château?
Château de Pray
Route de Charge
37400 Amboise
Tel: (47) 57 23 67

You will be living in a château which is part of the history of France and goes back to 1244. The château now belongs to the Farard family who supervise the hotel. Here you have got everything. Should you require a four poster bed and a life of splendour surrounded by antiques and oil paintings, this is for you. It has only 16 rooms so it is important that you book early. The food is of a very high standard, but as you would expect it is expensive.

Closed:	January and early February
Credit cards:	Visa
Rating:	★★★★

The Auberge du Mail
32 Quai Général-de-Gaulle
Amboise
Tel: (47) 57 60 39

This is a small restaurant on the riverfront just outside the town on the road to Tours. The food is of a very high standard. The speciality of the house is certainly Filet de Chevreuil sauce grand veneur (Roebuck with a currant sauce). Very good selection of local wines.

Closed:	November 15-30, March 1-15, Tuesday evenings
Rooms:	14
Credit cards:	AmEx, Diners, Visa
Rating:	★★★

Le Mail St Thomas
Place Richelieu
Amboise
Tel: (47) 57 22 52

Speciality of the house is Foie confit au Vouvray. This is like goose liver but it is not. Its recipe is a secret.

Credit cards:	AmEx, Diners, Visa
Rating:	★★★

USEFUL INFORMATION: AMBOISE

Postal Address:	37400 Indre-et-Loire
Population:	11,500
Distances:	Paris 210km, Blois 35km, Tours 25km.
Tourist Office:	Quai de Général de Gaulle Tel: (47) 57 09 28

Annual events:
Easter and August 15th: local wine fair (great fun)
First Wednesday in September: Melon Fair
Third Wednesday in November: Fair of St Catherine

DAY 7

Amboise, Chaumont-sur-Loire, Amboise: approx. 30 km (19 miles)

The day is primarily spent exploring Amboise, which means in particular visiting the château. There is also a short excursion to Chaumont-sur-Loire.

Overnight at Amboise.

Map references:
Amboise   1°00′E 47°25′N
Chaumont-sur-Loire   1°12′E 47°29′N

Route shown pp. 82.

An old wine press

Breakfast at Amboise.

After breakfast walk to the château, this is well signposted.

Gustave Flaubert wrote the following when he visited Amboise in 1847:

> The weather had become milder, the rain had stopped and the gentle evening sun welcomed us to Amboise. Here the streets are friendly as at Blois. People stand talking at their doors and work outside. The women-folk, who are almost all dark, have gentle faces and are extremely pretty. They are very feminine, with a benign voluptuousness.
>
> You are in the prosperous, gentle countryside of Touraine, the country of good white wine and fine old castles bordering the Loire, that most French of French rivers.
>
> The Castle of Amboise dominates the entire town, which seems scattered below it like a heap of pebbles round a rock. It has the imposing air of a fortress with its tall wide towers pierced by long, narrow semi-circular windows; its arcaded gallery joins the twin towers, the sombre colour of the walls contrasting starkly with the flowers above, like a bright plume on the bronzed head of an old soldier. We spent a good quarter of an hour admiring the tower on the left.
>
> We walked up to the castle along a gentle slope, which became a terrace with a mature garden. From the terrace there was a wonderful view over the surrounding gentle green countryside. Poplars lined the river banks and meadows retreated into the distance of the misty blue horizon, marked indistinctly by the outline of the hills. The Loire flowed through this landscape soaking the edges of the meadows, drifting around its islands. The mills were made to turn and the chains of boats slid through its meandering, silvery current, floating side by side, half asleep, obeying the command of the rudder. In the distance there were two large sails gleaming white in the sun.

This description so captures the atmosphere of Amboise even now that it could have been written yesterday.

The château of Amboise is the oldest in the Loire valley. There have been fortifications here since prehistoric times. It became strategically important during the Gallo-Roman period, when a bridge was built, providing the only river crossing in the area. In the 11th century the fortress was owned by the Counts of Amboise. They were continually fighting with the occupants of a fortress on the opposite (north) bank. The Counts of Amboise eventually won so their fortress continued to belong to the family until it was confiscated by Charles VII. He gave it to his step-daughter Charlotte of Savoy, the wife of Louis XI. It was here that Charles VIII was born and spent his childhood. He became very fond of Amboise and in 1492 he started work on a huge château of vast dimensions.

After campaigning in Italy, Charles brought back Italian artists, architects and gardeners, who introduced early Renaissance ideas. In 1498 Charles VIII hit his head on a low lintel, which resulted in his untimely death. After this further construction work came to a halt.

Louis XII preferred to live at Blois, he gave the château to Louise de Savoy, whose son was the future King François I. François came to Amboise when he was six. The court was there during the first three years of his reign. This was Amboise's Golden Age. François completed a wing begun by Louis XII, and he invited Leonardo da Vinci to come and live in the manor house of Clos-Lucé.

During the reign of Henry II the court moved to Blois. The last royal event here was one of horror. The château was the setting for one of the most tragic happenings in the history of France, during the short reign of the young King François II. A plot was hatched by Protestant agitators led by La Renaudie. They planned to go to Blois and ask the young King for permission to practice their religion and overthrow the powerful Catholic Guises, who were enemies of the Huguenots. The plot was revealed. As Blois was a difficult place to defend, the court moved to Amboise. The conspirators followed. When they arrived they were arrested. La Renaudie died fighting, his body was quartered and hung on the main gates of the town. The prisoners were hanged and swung on the battlements of the château, others were beheaded and hacked to pieces or thrown alive in sacks into the Loire.

Whilst I was in the course of writing this book, I was staying at the Hôtel du Lion d'Or, and my bedroom overlooked the walls of the château. They were trying out the Son-et-Lumière unbeknown to me and I woke startled as the floodlights came on with loud screams, and musket fire, to say the least I thought I was dreaming and reliving this frightful day in the history of Amboise.

After these terrible events, the Kings of France abandoned the château of Amboise. Louis XIII went there, but only on the occasional hunting expedition. He gave it to his brother Gaston d'Orléans and after his death it served as a state prison. It went through several hands after this, and eventually it became a prison again during the Revolution. The château was very badly damaged during the 1939-45 war but was restored and now belongs to the Saint-Louis Foundation.

As you look at the château's imposing exterior you must recall that the fortress which once stood on this site was demolished. The existing château was begun in 1465 with strategic and military objectives the major consideration. Larger windows were added at a later date, as well as Renaissance details which softened the original concept. So we see a medieval château perched high on a hill, with its turrets, drawbridge and generally feudal look, alleviated by the later additions.

I have not got space to guide you fully around the château but do see the exceptionally beautiful St Hubert chapel. This was built towards the end of the 15th century, in the Flamboyant style, and it is highly possible that Leonardo da Vinci is buried here. The stag's antlers on the spire represent St Hubert, the patron saint of hunting.

The château is open throughout the year, 9am-noon, 2pm-7pm (in winter 5.30pm).

Now, how about a cup of coffee at Bigot's?

Lunch at Amboise

After lunch in one of the many little restaurants in the town, you could visit the Postal Museum. This is situated at 6 rue Joyeuse. It houses probably the most important collection of memorabilia relating to postal services in France. You will see the first French postage stamp printed in 1849, a most fascinating exhibition. Open April-September 9.30am-noon, 2pm-6.30pm; October-March 10am-noon, 2pm-5pm. Note that it is closed Tuesdays and Bank Holidays.

I recommend a short drive to Chaumont, the return trip is only 30 km (about 19 miles). Take the D751 to Chaumont-sur-Loire.

Chaumont-sur-Loire

Upon your arrival, park by the riverside and walk into the village. The château is well worth looking at from the outside. Note: it closes at 6.30pm I am not quite sure about the château of Chaumont. Sometimes it stands proud and majestic above the village, and sometimes it looks grim, this depends on the angle you look at it and the weather. Perhaps it is its history that has an effect on me, because it is here that Catherine de Medici entertained her cronies, all those astrologers and magicians, who helped and guided her in endeavouring to put spells on anyone who stood in her way. As I mentioned before, she had her eye on Chenonceaux, but her husband gave it to Diane de Poitiers and Catherine had Chaumont, but she did have her own way in the end, when she became Regent, see p. 77. Catherine proposed to the former regal favourite, that she should exchange Chenonceaux for Chaumont. This was no request, it was an order and Diane had no choice but to exchange her pleasant home for this stern fortress. In fact Diane lived for only a short time at Chaumont, where everything presumably reminded her of her rival. She left to live in her château at Anet, where she died.

Inside you can see the rooms of the two rivals, Catherine de Medici and Diane de Poitiers and the astrologer Ruggien's study. You can also view the magnificent stables and saddlery, built in the nineteenth century.

It was at Chaumont that Henry II met Thomas à Becket for the last time.

Return to Amboise on the same road. You may wish to stop at one of the many caves serving wines from Touraine along the roadside.

Remember there is a Son-et-Lumière at the château in the evening during the season under the title 'Royal Castle of Amboise'. This is performed on a Wednesday and Saturday night and starts at 9pm. It is created, produced and performed by the people of Amboise and neighbouring villages (420 people in total). It is quite a spectacle, fireworks, lights, sound effects . . . You will walk out feeling as though you have actually lived in those days. If you are there on a day when it is performed, do not miss it.

Dinner and overnight at Amboise.

View of the Loire, with punts

DAY 8

Amboise, Vouvray, Blois: approx. 68km (43 miles).

Leave in good time. The journey is not long, but there is a lot to see and do, starting with an interesting visit to the caves of Vouvray.

You will arrive in Blois in time for lunch. As there are so many restaurants and a great variety of them, I leave the choice to you, but keep it simple as I have recommended a gourmet meal for the evening.

Afternoon visit to the château and the town.

Overnight at Blois.

Map references:

Amboise	1°00′E 47°25′N
Vouvray	0°48′E 47°26′N
Blois	1°20′E 47°35′N

Route shown p. 82.

Breakfast at Amboise

After an excellent breakfast and lashings of coffee, cross the town bridge in Amboise and continue through the town on the other side of the river Loire to Nazelles Négron. Turn left onto the D1, through Noizay and Vernou-sur-Brenne, to join the D46 to Vouvray.

Vouvray

Vouvray is a pleasant village, known throughout the world for its excellent wine. There are two grapes cultivated here, the wine is made either from Pineau blanc or Chenin which is a common vine in the Loire valley. The vineyards cover 4,500 acres, all situated around the village.

Drive through the village and you will see many caves. A good one to visit would be the Cave Cooperative des Grands Vins, it is well signposted, but there are also many smaller ones. Here you can sample the wine, purchase a few bottles to take home or consume on a picnic later on your holiday. The small producers are wonderful, I remember one morning in April buying from a very old lady who had lived in Vouvray all her life. Her late husband had won many prizes for his wine, certificates and rosettes covered the walls of her cave.

There are three types of wine grown locally. Still, slightly effervescent known as 'Petillant', and the famous sparkling wine made in the same way as champagne (Méthode Champenoise). These wines range from extra dry through to sweet. So you have got a wide choice. Vouvray is a fruity and light wine, and the beauty is that you can keep it for many years. As you raise your glass remember the motto of Vouvray which is 'It'll warm the cockles of your heart' (Célà suffit à réchauffer le coeur même). There is no wine museum here, but on the fourth weekend in January there is a wine fair.

Leave Vouvray on the N152. Return along the north side of the Loire past Amboise (give it a salute), through Veuves. Continue past Chaumont-sur-Loire, again on the other side of the river, through Chouzy-sur-Cisse to Blois.

Blois

As you approach Blois on the N152 you will see L'Espérance restaurant, make a note of it as you may return in the evening. Blois is a busy town, with excellent shops, although they can be of Paris standards and Paris prices.

Lunch at Blois

After lunch, proceed to the château, where we are back with Catherine de Medici again. You will enjoy the walk up winding streets and there it is, in all its majesty high above the river and the town. A very beautiful stately château whose history abounds with incident. It is a fine example of the architecture of France through from the 13th century to the 17th century.

As you enter the courtyard you are struck by the great variety of complex detail and structure, mainly due to the enthusiastic contributions lavished on it by two great kings, Louis XII and François I. Everywhere you look you can see the carvings of their emblems decorating the extensions which they added to the original feudal fortress. The emblem of Louis XII is the porcupine, and that of François I, the salamander. It was at this fortress that Joan of Arc arranged for her soldiers to take Communion before leaving for Orléans, having first driven away all the loose camp followers.

Charles d'Orléans, who spent 25 years of his life in captivity in England, wrote poetry and dreamt about his childhood in Blois. When he eventually returned, he set about turning it into a more comfortable place to live in. His son became Louis XII, known as the 'Father of the People'. It was Louis' favourite château and it was also a favourite of his second wife Anne de Bretagne. Together they added a new wing. François de Prontriand was in charge, later he was one of the team responsible for Chambord. You will see the equestrian statue of Louis XII standing over the late gothic entrance with the porcupine beneath, the heraldic ermine with it was Anne's. After Anne died he made a last attempt to provide an heir by marrying Mary, the sister of Henry VIII in 1514, when she was 16 years of age. However he died 11 weeks after the marriage, and his cousin François I ascended to the throne at the age of 20 in 1515. François was a great patron of the arts. He was inspired by the Renaissance in Italy, and ordered the construction of another wing, opposite Louis XII's. Part of his achievement is a world-renowned exterior spiral staircase with ornate balconies where courtiers could watch tournaments in the courtyard. Note the salamander symbols.

There is so much of interest to see inside. Every room is steeped in history. The overall impression is one of great richness. The walls and beams are decorated with intricate designs in gold and glowing colours, all carefully restored.

The room of Catherine de Medici is intriguing, it has 237 carved wooden panels, with secret compartments. What did this formidable lady hide in them, jewels and poisons perhaps. You will also see the room where the famous murder took place of the Duc de Guise, by the order of Catherine's son, Henry III. The power and ambitions of the Guise family had been fueled by their recent successes during the Wars of Religion (see p. 22) and Henry III sensed that his throne was threatened by the strength of the Catholic League, headed by Henry de Guise. He therefore decided to do away with Henry and also his brother the Cardinal of Lorraine.

On Christmas Eve 1588, Charlotte de Sauves, Henry de Guise's mistress, was handed two notes, warning of a plot against his life. Henry dismissed them with a laugh and proceeded to the opening of the King's Council.

The King had chosen a group of men to do the deed. The first blow was struck by Montseriac, then the others leapt on their victim, and he was stabbed by them all. On the same day the Cardinal of Lorraine was executed. Both bodies were burned and the ashes thrown in the Loire.

Henry IV's second wife, Marie de Medici was exiled to Blois after his death. Thereafter the importance of Blois began to decline.

In 1628 Louis XIII's brother Gaston inherited the château. His object was to rebuild it but he ran out of money (thank goodness), leaving only the incomplete Gaston d'Orléans wing which now houses the town's library. After Gaston left this world, Blois once again reverted to a royal residence. Louis XIV was not particularly interested in it and gave it to Jean Sobieski, the widow of a Polish hero, a rather strange thing to happen in my estimation. Now along came Louis XV who decided that the whole place should be demolished (obviously he had no taste), but fortunately the army wanted it for a barracks. The town of Blois acquired it in 1810, but the army still remained in residence after this.

In 1944 it was badly damaged in the war, but a wonderful job of reconstruction has been carried out. It now houses the Museum of Fine Arts as well as an archaeological museum. You will enjoy your tour around the château, look out for my friend Catherine de Medici as she is everywhere.

The château is open from April to the end of August from 9am-6.30pm. The rest of the year from 9am-noon, 2pm-5pm. Son-et-Lumière in the evening during the season. Details and times you can get from your hotel.

Return to your hotel and afterwards walk around the town and you will find a large choice of nice restaurants for dinner (I have made a couple of suggestions below), or you may return to l'Espérance.

Dinner and overnight at Blois.

USEFUL INFORMATION: BLOIS

Population:	49,500
Postal Address:	4100 Loire-et-Cher
Railway station:	Tel: (54) 78 50 50
Tourist Office:	Pavilion Anne de Bretagne
	3 Avenue Jean-Laigret
	Tel: (54) 74 06 49

La Péniche
Promenade du Mail
Blois
Tel: (54) 74 37 23

Would you like to dine on a barge on the Loire? If so, try this. It specialises in local cuisine and is known for its seasonal fresh fare.

Open all year
Credit cards: AmEx, Diners, Visa
Rating: ★★

Rendez-vous des Pêcheurs
27 Rue du Foix
Blois
Tel: (54) 74 67 48

A charming little restaurant.

Credit cards: Visa
Rating: ★★

L'Espérance
189 Quai Ulysee-Besnard
Blois (a mile from the centre of town)
Tel: (54) 78 09 01

A very beautiful restaurant, with breathtaking views of the surrounding countryside. Have you ever had truffled omelette? If not now is your chance. Prices are reasonable but the à la carte can be expensive.

Closed:	February, Sunday evenings, Mondays
Credit cards:	All major cards
Rating:	★★★★

Hôtel Urbis
3 rue Porte-Côte
Blois
Tel: (54) 74 01 17

This is part of the famous Urbis (and Ibis) group of hotels. It is modern, the rooms are well-equipped and tastefully decorated. It is situated in the centre of the town. Although there is no restaurant, it is in easy reach of many. Ideal for the family, you are very close to the shops and the château. Prices are reasonable, and there are special rates for children.

Rooms:	55
Credit cards:	All major cards
Rating:	★★★

Anne de Bretagne
31 Avenue J-Laigret (close to the railway station)
Blois
Tel: (54) 78 05 38

A lovely restful hotel. The prices are reasonable. Unfortunately it has not got a restaurant, but again there are plenty available in the town.

Rooms:	29
Credit cards:	All major cards
Rating:	★★★

DAY 9

Blois, Chambord, Beaugency: approx. 48 km (30 miles)

After breakfast, strolling and shopping in the old part of the town.

The journey to Chambord should take about 45 minutes, so leave in time to have lunch there. Then you will be ready to spend the afternoon visiting the château and grounds. The journey to Beaugency is through lovely wooded countryside. It is not a long drive, but aim to get there early in the evening.

Overnight at Beaugency.

Map references:
Blois   1°20′E 47°35′N
Chambord   1°31′E 47°37′N
Beaugency   1°38′E 47°48′N

Route shown pp. 82.

Breakfast in Blois.

After breakfast have a quiet stroll around the town, possibly do a little shopping.

Leave Blois by crossing the old bridge and turn immediately left onto the D951. Follow the river as far as Montlivault, and turn right on the D84.

Chambord

You are now in Chambord, where an experience of a lifetime awaits you, for among those who love the châteaux of the Loire, Chambord is considered the king of châteaux.

Lunch at Chambord

To visit the château you enter through the park, acre after acre of forest and woodland, and before you, you will see the hunting lodge of François I. It is magnificent and enormous containing 440 rooms in total. When I first saw it many years ago, I was particularly struck by the whiteness of the stone, contrasted by the inset slate patterns, which ornament hosts of towers, lanterns, turrets and chimneys, it seemed to me to resemble a great wedding cake.

The château is most impressive in the early morning as the mist rises or in the evening as the sun sets. The whole of Chambord and the estate belongs to the French nation, and as far as I know this is the only one that does. The woods are full of animals and birds, boar, ducks, deer and birds of prey. In the forest you will find observation towers where you can watch the animals from a safe distance. Later (Day 11, p. 121) you will visit the terrific Hunting Museum at Gien, where there are documents showing the daily total of animals killed on the hunts held at Chambord. As it belongs to the Nation, the President has the right to shoot on this land, and at the Museum you will see invitation cards from past Presidents inviting well known people to shooting weekends. Without these shoots, the forests of Chambord could not contain all this wild life.

The park, properly called the Parc National d'Elevage et Réserve Cynegetique (National Hunting Reserve and Breeding Park) is 13,600 acres in total, within which lies woodland amounting to 11,100 acres. A wall, the longest in France, totalling 20 miles surrounds it. You can take a ride in a horse-drawn carriage around the grounds should you so wish.

To see the château reflected in the waters of the Grand Canal really is a sight. If you sit here in the evening light, you will find it a wonderful place to meditate on what life is all about, the peace and tranquillity are beyond words. As you sit and look at the château you can imagine what it was like in the reign of François I, when Chambord was the hunting lodge on which he lavished so much enthusiasm. Imagine the wild parties, members of the Court jostling for position, it is better than any film set.

While staying in Blois François I decided to build a castle where he could participate in his favourite occupation, hunting. Chambord proved the ideal spot, with its forests and wildlife. Work started in 1519, and it is pretty certain that Leonardo da Vinci had been consulted in the earlier planning stage. The Keep was finished in 1535 and the Royal Apartments about 1550. François I was devoted to this building until the day he died. Sadly he never saw its final completion.

After his death Henry II tried to finish the château. You will see his emblem, a capital H and a crescent, on a staircase in the courtyard, as well as in the second storey of the Chapel and the adjoining wing. Catherine de Medici enjoyed visits here in the company of her son Charles XI, who apparently thrived on the excitement of the hunt.

Henri IV and Louis XIII appeared to show no interest in Chambord, but when Louis XIV came to the throne work started again. It was badly mauled in the Revolution and afterwards became State property. Believe it or not, only in 1947 did Chambord come back into its own, after extensive renovations had been carried out.

Enjoy your trip around the château, the highlight of the tour you will find is the two-way Grand Staircase. This is fascinating, and I feel sure that Leonardo had a hand in it, it has his stamp.

As you enter the building, there it is, in the centre under the lantern dome. Supported on eight pillars, it is an open work construction with balustrades. The two spirals wind around a central post. As you climb the great staircase, you will see others coming down, but you will not pass them. This magnificent staircase needs to be experienced to be fully appreciated. It leads to each floor and the terraces. Here is a wonderworld of charm. You are right on top amongst skylights, pinnacles, the four pavilions and the great tall chimneys with the magnificent lantern dome in the middle. It is all lavishly decorated. You can touch the inset motifs in slate and get close to the salamanders of monumental size, topped with royal crowns.

Inside the building there is much to discover. In fact there are 440 rooms, 14 great staircases and 70 secondary staircases. However it is all so spacious and well planned, that it is easy to find your way about. Each apartment is clearly documented.

On the ground floor you will find the François I Hunting Room and the Sun Room with interesting paintings. On the first floor there are the Royal Bedchamber, the François I tower and the Queen's Suite, all containing paintings, tapestries and furniture to delight the eye. The second floor is devoted to the hunt, where you will find animal paintings and items of interest related to the sport.

The château is open: July and August 9.30am-noon, 2pm-7pm. It closes at 6pm April-June, September and October, and at 5pm for the rest of the year.

As you would expect there is Son-et-Lumière during the high season. Details of performance times are available from the Tourist Office.

There is a parade of shops selling all types of souvenirs, normally I cannot stand this form of commercialism but this has been tastefully done and it does not jar on the landscape. At one end there is a good self-service restaurant offering a varied choice of food at reasonable prices.

Leave Chambord on the D33. Drive slowly as you will be going through the forest, drink in the beauty, and who knows perhaps you will see a wild boar (unless he sees you first). This may be a good place to make this statement. Every year whilst I am living in France I read in the local papers that some motorist has collided with a wild boar. Late at night this can be nasty, nobody in the UK believes me, but I can assure you it is true.

Go through Thoury and Crouy-sur-Cosson, then the road becomes the D103. You drive through lovely wooded countryside to La Ferté-St Cyr. Just as you enter the village you turn left onto the D925.

You are now on the road to Beaugency. This is a lovely drive, look out for butterflies, we saw so many in the month of July.

Beaugency

When you arrive in Beaugency cross the old bridge and turn left along the quai, lined with plane trees. Proceed up the hill following the 'Centre Ville' signs.

Beaugency has some interesting landmarks, one of the most picturesque is the Rivulet. The street has a stream running down the middle and, decked in flowers, it really is beautiful. To get there just stroll to the left of the charming Renaissance Town Hall, which is in the old district of the town, you will find Pouet-Chaumont Lane, you proceed down the steps and then you reach the rue de Pont. About 100 yards to your left you will find the rue du Ru (the Rivulet).

You may wish to walk down to the Château Dunois (15th-century). Dunois was the bastard son of Louis XI, Duke of Orléans, who bought him home as a baby to be reared by his wife with the rest of the family. He became a great soldier: Joan of Arc owed a lot of her success to the support of Dunois. He built the château in 1440. Now it is a museum of the art and traditions of Orléanais.

Note also the Abbey Church of Our Lady (Église Abbatiale Nôtre Dame). This 12th-century Romanesque building was where the marriage of Eleanor of Aquitaine and Louis VII was declared null and void, because she had failed to provide him with a son. Eight weeks after the annulment she married Henry II of England. She gave Henry five boys and three girls in fifteen years.

Dinner and overnight at Beaugency.

Hôtel du Grand Michel
103 Place Saint-Michel
Chambord
Tel: (54) 20 31 31

Should you wish to have a full lunch this very pleasant hotel is in the grounds close by the château. Here you can get an excellent lunch either in the dining room or outside with wonderful views of the château. The restaurant specialises in regional dishes. Prices are reasonable.

Closed:	Mid-November-mid-December. Restaurant closed Monday evenings and Tuesdays out of season
Rooms:	38
Credit cards:	Visa
Rating:	★★

There is another restaurant in the grounds of Chambord:

Le Relais-Bernard Robin
Chambord
Tel: (54) 46 41 22

This is a good restaurant of a very high standard, again it specialises in regional dishes and wines. The prices are a little on the high side, but the food is excellent. A good place to have lunch if it is your birthday or you wish to celebrate something of importance.

Credit cards:	none accepted

Hostellerie de l'Ecu de Bretagne
Place du Martroi
Beaugency
Tel: (38) 44 67 60

This is a good family hotel in the main square, the bedrooms are comfortable and well appointed. The dining room is spacious and there are three set menus for dinner, which certainly posed a problem as far as I was concerned. Which one should I choose, I kept saying to myself. All three were good and all contained local regional dishes. Try the Cul de Lapereau au Miel (Rabbit cooked in honey). M. Conan the owner tells me that this is what his hotel is known for, and I think I believe him.

There is a very pleasant bar where you can have a drink before dinner and this is also where breakfast is served.

Now my dear reader, I say again, please book before your holiday. This is a popular hotel, especially with people travelling to the south of the country, who find it a comfortable overnight stop.

Closed:	January 25-March 1
Rooms:	26
Facilities:	Restaurant, parking
Credit cards:	All major cards
Rating:	★★★

Hôtel de la Sologne
Place St Firmin
Beaugency
Tel: (38) 44 50 27

This is a good family hotel, very comfortable, there is a lovely winter garden which is nice to relax in on a cool evening.

Rooms:	16
Facilities:	No restaurant, rooms with television and telephone
Credit cards:	All major cards
Rating:	★★★

L'Abbaye de Beaugency
2 Quai de l'Abbaye
Beaugency
Tel: (38) 44 67 35

This is a first class hotel, 17th-century, and stands in a wonderful position above the old bridge, overlooking the river. As you would expect it is a little expensive. The rooms are superb and there are 5 suites.

The food is of a very high standard and if the weather is hot you can dine outside as well, with terrific views of our dear friend the river Loire.

Should you wish to stay in this fine establishment, the prices are high but so is the class of service you will receive and also the food.

Open all year
Rooms: 13
Facilities: TV and telephones in all rooms,
                    good parking
Credit cards: all major cards
Rating: ★★★★

USEFUL INFORMATION: BEAUGENCY

Postal address: 45190 Loiret
Population: 7,000
Altitude: 106m
Distances: Paris 140km, Blois 30km
Tourist Office: 28 Place du Martroi
                    Tel: (38) 44 54 42
                    (Note: closed on Sunday)
Annual events:
June: Antique Fair
September: Wine Fair
If you are in Beaugency on a Saturday there is a great open market with fruit, vegetables, cheese, meat, live chickens, flowers and crafts.

DAY 10

Beaugency to Orléans: approx. 28 km (17 miles)

Today you have a choice of destination, either Orléans or Sully-sur-Loire. The main route takes us direct to Orléans for a day spent exploring this city, made famous for most of us by Joan of Arc. However, for those who prefer to avoid the bustle of a large metropolis whilst on holiday I have detailed a day's trip to Sully-sur-Loire across country on quiet roads through woodlands interspersed with lakes and little flower-decked villages.

Overnight at Orléans (detour, overnight Sully-sur-Loire).

Map references:

Beaugency	1°38′E 47°46′N
Cléry St André	1°45′E 47°49′N
Orléans	1°55′E 47°54′N

Detour

La Ferté-St Aubin	1°57′E 47°43′N
Sennely	2°09′E 47°41′N
Sully-sur-Loire	2°23′E 47°47′N

Route shown p. 118.

Breakfast at Beaugency.

Leave Beaugency by crossing the bridge southwards onto the D19. The road is lined with acacias. When you reach Lailly-en-Val turn left onto the D951, signposted Orléans.

At this point you may choose to detour across to Sully-sur-Loire (see p. 112).

Cléry St André

Make a stop at Cléry St André, Louis XI was interred in the Church of Notre Dame. This church was on the main pilgrims' route as they travelled south towards the shrine of St James in Compostella, Spain.

The pilgrims stopped here to see a statue of the Virgin and Child, which was discovered by a ploughman in 1280. It became a cult and a larger church was built to accommodate the pilgrims, but it was destroyed in 1428 by the Earl of Salisbury. Charles VII gave money towards building a new church. Louis XI and his son Charles XIII continued to support the construction. The church was begun in Gothic style at the east end, but completed in Renaissance style by the time they reached the west end. The statue is still here, covered by a mantle, and there is also a monument to Louis XI. It is well worth looking at the misericords under the seats in the choir. They were donated by Henry II.

Continue on the D951, drive over the A10 motorway, turn left in about 2 miles to cross the old bridge into the town centre. You are now in Orléans.

Orléans

Orléans was badly damaged during World War II but it has been very carefully rebuilt, and even though it does not look quite like it did during the life of Joan of Arc, it is nevertheless a very interesting town to visit. It is the main town of the district of Loiret and spreads over both banks of the Loire.

Lunch at Orléans.

The main reason why people visit Orléans is because of Joan of Arc, as she is well-known for relieving the town in 1429 from the English (see p. 17) and she has certainly become the adopted daughter of the town. In the Place du Martroi you will find a most impressive equestrian statue of her, well worth a visit.

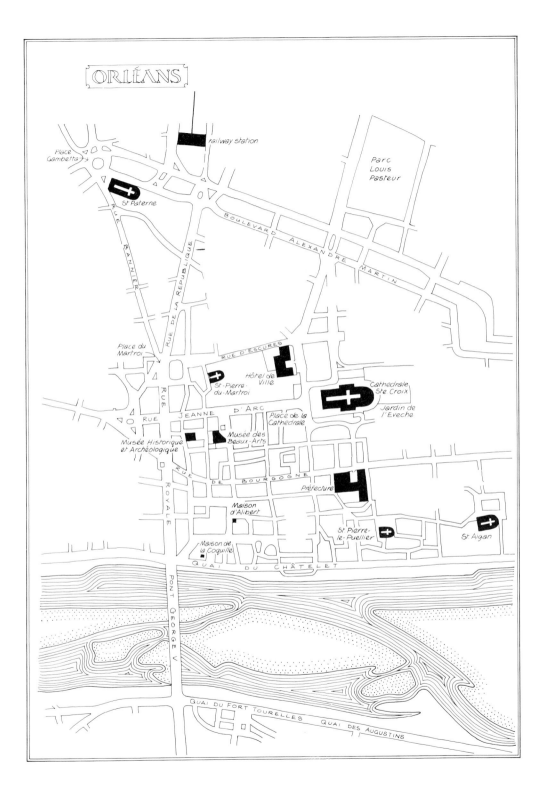

ORLÉANS

railway station

Place Gambetta

St Paterne

Parc Louis Pasteur

BOULEVARD ALEXANDRE MARTIN

RUE BANNIER

RUE DE LA RÉPUBLIQUE

RUE D'ESCURES

Place du Martroi

Hôtel de Ville

St-Pierre-du-Martroi

Cathédrale Ste Croix

RUE JEANNE D'ARC

Jardin de l'Évêché

Place de la Cathédrale

RUE ROYALE

Musée Historique et Archéologique

Musée des Beaux-Arts

RUE DE BOURGOGNE

Préfecture

Maison d'Alibert

St Pierre-le-Puellier

St Aignan

Maison de la Coquille

QUAI DU CHÂTELET

PONT GEORGE V

QUAI DU FORT TOURELLES   QUAI DES AUGUSTINS

Visit the rue Royale, which is close to the Place du Martroi. This was completely rebuilt in the 18th century. Then cross the Pont George V, on the other side a simple cross marks the place where Joan captured the Fort des Tourelles.

In the centre of the town stands the Ste-Croix Cathedral. Building started in 1287 in the high Gothic period, but it was burnt down by the Huguenots in 1568. It was rebuilt, two 16th-century arches of the original Cathedral had remained intact after the fire, and these were used as a model for the remainder of the Cathedral which explains its apparent unity of style. Henry IV laid the first stone for the new building in 1601 and it was eventually finished in 1829.

To note in particular are the 18th-century panelling in the choir and a most wonderful 17th-century organ, plus the Treasure Room with its Byzantine enamels and works in gold dating back to the 15th century.

Next, visit the Fine Arts Museum (the Musée des Beaux-Arts) in the Place de la Cathédrale. Here you will find a most wonderful collection of paintings, pastels and busts from the 15th to the 19th century. It is said that some of these paintings once hung in the château of Richelieu. Works exhibited include Houdon, Pigalle, Corrège, Le Nain among many others — but amid such a rich collection do not miss 'L'Ombre' by Rodin and 'St Thomas' by Velasquez. The museum opens daily 10am-noon; 2pm-6pm. It closes on Tuesday (tel: (38) 53 33 22).

Overnight at Orléans.

Detour

Leave Beaugency by crossing the bridge southwards onto the D19. The road is lined with acacias. Continue through Lailly-en-Val and on through gentle countryside to the D103. Take the left fork signposted Jouy-le-Potier and La Ferté-St Aubin. Drive through woodland to Jouy-le-Potier, turn left in the middle of the village and then turn immediately right by the church on to the D18. This is a quiet road which passes under a busy autoroute. There are lakes on your left hand side, just some of many in the area. At the road junction turn right into La Ferté-St Aubin.

The château of La Ferté-St Aubin is 17th-century and it has an outstanding animal park. You can visit the interior of the château — the rooms are fully furnished, there are even place settings in the dining room. In the extensive grounds there is a small model farm, while the animal park has roaming deer, ponies, and goats. In good weather this is a splendid place to stop for a picnic (although there is a cafeteria and tea room available).

Back in the town, turn onto the D17 (very easy to find because you turn left round the church, which is on the corner of the road — it has a very tall tower and this makes a good landmark as it is in view all the time you drive through the town). You are now back in cool wooded areas, and if you are travelling in the autumn you will see the rich colour of the trees and the heather. Again there are many lakes, like Chambord this is another excellent hunting area. Drive on to Ménestreau-en-Villette. This is a very pretty village, and has good parking should you wish to stop for a cooling drink or a coffee, and should you require a meal you will find the menu very reasonable at the Café de l'Union. Continue on the D17 to Sennely.

This again is a very beautiful little village, flowers everywhere. Easy parking should you wish to stop and there is also another little café called Auberge du Cerf with very reasonable prices and they have regional dishes on their menu. Turn left by the boulangerie. Look out for the signpost to Vannes (D120) which is situated in a flower bed. This is a long straight road through more woods and lakes. At the T-junction turn left onto the D83 signposted to Vannes-sur-Cosson. At the next junction take the D120 signposted to Sully-sur-Loire. Continue through the lake-studded woodlands with occasional farm dwellings to Viglain. Enter the village continuing on the D120, leave by the D320 to the D59, signposted Sully-sur-Loire.

When you arrive in Sully-sur-Loire follow 'Centre Ville' signs and park by the river and the château. The château is well signposted. Sully-sur-Loire is a very busy little town, it has a market each week which covers all the outlying villages.

The real beauty of this 14th- to 17th-century château lies in its architecture (which you can best see from the outside) with its turrets, pinnacles and machicolations reflected in the moat. There was a frightful fire here at the beginning of this century, and then it was very badly damaged again in World War II. The Department of the Loiret restored the château in 1962. Joan of Arc visited Sully in 1429 and talked Charles VII into going to Reims to make himself King of France. Voltaire spent a considerable amount of time at Sully. Only part of the château is open to the public, this being the wing of the castle that was built in the 14th century. It is celebrated for its painted ceilings.

The château is open May to September, 9am-noon, 2pm-6pm; October to April 10am-noon, 2pm-5pm. The château is spectacularly floodlit at night.

Overnight at Sully-sur-Loire

La Crémaillière
34 rue N-D-de-Recouvrance
Orléans
Tel: (38) 53 49 17

This is one of the finest restaurants in the whole of the Loire valley. The chef, Paul Huyart, is known throughout France. Needless to say the food is superb. It specialises in fish dishes such as Ragout of Scallops in Oysters (when in season), but there are other wonderful examples of the culinary art such as Fresh Duckling foie gras, Soufflé aux fruits, but the real must is his soup, Strawberries with Passion Fruit.

There is a first class wine list concentrating on the wines of the region: Sancerre and Menetou-Salon and the favourite of the house — Quincy.

Closed:	August, Sunday and Monday evenings
Credit cards:	AmEx, Diners, Visa
Rating:	★★★★

About a mile from the town centre on the road to Blois (N152) is this delightful auberge:

Auberge de la Montespan
Rue de Blois
Orléans
Tel: (38) 88 12 07

It is situated on the banks of the Loire, with a garden and terrace. You must try the Loire Salmon which is a speciality of the house, and also the Game Pâté. The restaurant is under the supervision of M. Fournier who is always at hand to guide you through the menu. There are 8 bedrooms which are very well apppointed and there is a delightful view of the Loire from the rooms.

Closed:	December 23-January 31
Credit cards:	Visa
Rating:	★★

La Poutrière
8-10 rue de la Breche
Orléans
Tel: (38) 66 02 30

It is advisable to book, as this is a very popular restaurant. The Chef Marcel Thomas, was originally a senior chef on the liner *France*. Salmon is one of the prominent dishes. Salmon in puff pastry, and salmon with black pepper and watercress sauce. There is, however, a good selection of meat dishes.

Closed:	March 1-8, Sunday evening, Mondays
Credit cards:	AmEx, Diners, Visa
Rating:	★★★

Sofitel Orléans
44-6 Quai Barentin
Orléans
Tel: (38) 62 17 39

This hotel has an excellent restaurant specialising in local regional food. It must be stated that this is a grand hotel with every comfort, which is reflected in the prices. But should you wish a night of luxury, this is your hotel.

Open all year
Rooms:	108
Facilities:	Swimming pool, parking
Credit cards:	AmEx, Diners, Visa
Rating:	★★★★

Hôtel St Martin
52 Boulevard A-Martin
Orléans
Tel: (38) 62 47 47

This is a very pleasant small hotel close to the Cathedral.

Hôtel St Martin cont'd

Closed:	December 24-January 3
Rooms:	22
Facilities:	no restaurant
Credit cards:	Visa
Rating:	★★

Hostellerie du Grand Sully
10, bd du Champ-de-Foire
Sully-sur-Loire
Tel: (38) 36 27 56

A very small, quiet hotel. Lovely restaurant, at very reasonable prices, with local food beautifully cooked. Remember to book in advance as accommodation is limited in Sully-sur-Loire.

Closed:	Hotel, December 20-January 15
	Restaurant, Mondays October-
	31 March
Rooms:	12
Credit cards:	AmEx, Diners, Visa
Rating:	★★

Le Pont de Sologne
21 rue Porte-de-Sologne
Sully-sur-Loire
Tel: (38) 36 26 34

Rooms:	25
Facilities:	Restaurant
Rating:	★★

USEFUL INFORMATION: ORLÉANS

Postal Address:	45000 Loiret
Population:	105,000
Altitude:	116m
Distances:	Blois 56km; Bourges 105km; Paris 116km; Le Mans 138km
Tourist Office:	Place Albert Tel: (38) 53 05 95 (Closed Sundays, out of season. Information can also be obtained from the Town Hall)
Town Hall:	Place de l'Etape Tel: (38) 42 22 22 (open 15 April-15 September)

Annual Events:
January: Instrumental festival
May 8: Festival of Joan of Arc
December: Musical Week
There is an Antique Market every Saturday at the Bld Alexander-Martin. Food Market in the Market Hall every day except Monday.

USEFUL INFORMATION: SULLY-SUR-LOIRE

Postal Address:	45600 Loiret
Population:	5,825
Distances:	Paris 139km, Bourges 82km, Orléans 48km
Facilities:	Golf course
Tourist Office:	place Générale de Gaulle Tel: (38) 36 23 70

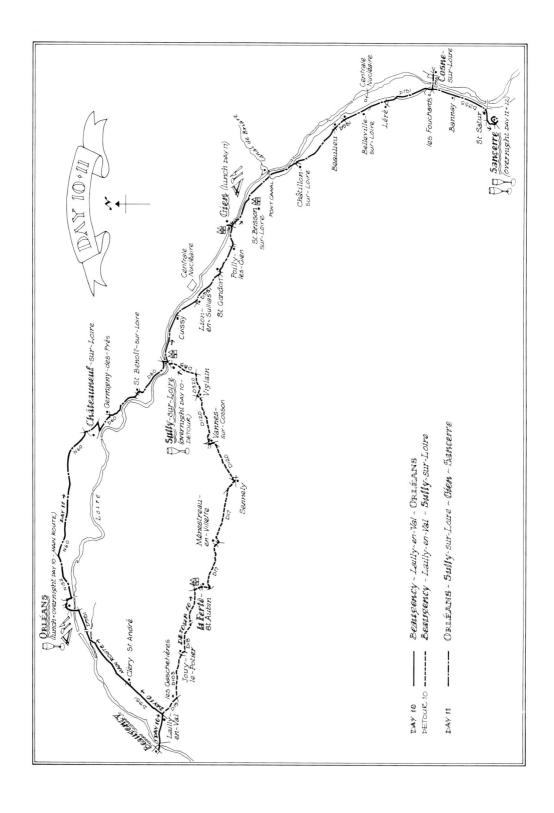

DAY 10 ⋄ 11

Orléans
(lunch~overnight DAY 10 ~ MAIN ROUTE)

Cléry St André

Lailly~
en~Val

Beaugency

Jouy~
le~Potier

la Ferté~
St Aubin

Ménestreau~
en~Villette

Sennely

Vannes~
sur~Cosson

Viglain

Sully~sur~Loire
(overnight DAY 10~
DETOUR)

Germigny~des~Prés

Châteauneuf~sur~Loire

St Benoît~sur~Loire

Cuissy

Centrale
Nucléaire

Lion~
en~Sullias

St Gondon

Poilly~
les~Gien

St Brisson
sur~Loire

Gien (lunch DAY 11)

PONT CANAL

Châtillon~
sur~Loire

Beaulieu

Belleville~
sur~Loire

Centrale
Nucléaire

Léré

les Fouchards

Cosne~
sur~Loire

Bannay

St Satur

Sancerre
(overnight DAY 11~ 12)

DAY 10 ————— Beaugency ~ Lailly~en~Val ~ Orléans

DETOUR 10 - - - - - Beaugency ~ Lailly~en~Val ~ Sully~sur~Loire

DAY 11 —·—·—·— Orléans ~ Sully~sur~Loire ~ Gien ~ Sancerre

DAY 11

Orléans, Châteauneuf-sur-Loire, Sully-sur-Loire, Gien, Sancerre:
approx. 115 km (72 miles).

In the morning you travel southwest to visit first the Musée de la Marine de la
Loire in Châteauneuf-sur-Loire, and then you will certainly want to break your
journey at St Benôit-sur-Loire to visit the abbey church. After visiting Sully-sur-
Loire (where those who took yesterday's detour rejoin the main route), we
continue along the Loire to Gien for lunch, then on to Sancerre.

Overnight at Sancerre

Map references:
Orléans	1°55'E 47°54'N
Châteauneuf-sur-Loire	2°14'E 47°53'N
Sully-sur-Loire	2°23'E 47°47'N
Gien	2°38'E 47°41'N
Sancerre	2°50'E 47°20'N

Breakfast at Orléans

Leave Orléans by the N60, this is a busy fast road that will take you in the direction of Châteauneuf-sur-Loire. In about 28km you will come to a major crossroads. Turn right onto the D952 and almost immediately left into Châteauneuf-sur-Loire. There is a parking area by the château gates.

Châteauneuf-sur-Loire

This small town suffered damage during the last war but, like so many French towns, it has been rebuilt as it was before. The château is 17th-century. Sadly a greater part of it was demolished by an unappreciative owner after the Revolution. There is a fascinating museum here now. The Musée de la Marine de la Loire is worth a visit for those interested in the navigation of the Loire in times past — the exhibits include not only early sailing tackle, huge anchors, etc, but also offers insights into the lives of the mariners.

Open daily 10am-11.45am, and 2pm-4.45pm. Closed December until the end of February.

Drive through the town and take the D60 on your right passing through Germigny-des-Prés, then follow the riverside to St Benôit-sur-Loire.

St Benôit-sur-Loire

This village is clustered around an old abbey church. It was once the abbey of Fleury, founded in the 7th century. The second Abbot heard that the abbey of Monte Cassino in Italy had been wrecked by the Lombards, so he sent a small and daring party of monks on a seven-hundred-mile journey to recover the bones of St Benedict. When the relics were installed, the abbey changed its name to St Benôit. It soon became one of the great centres of learning, famed for its scribes and scholars. It not only attracted pilgrims but also Norsemen, who raided it. In 1026 a fire destroyed the church. Rebuilding began immediately and resulted in one of the finest abbey churches in the Loire valley. The abbey's glorious years were interrupted when it was sacked by the Huguenots and after the Revolution it was closed down completely.

In 1944 the present community of monks moved in. They are working to restore the buildings and the spiritual life of the abbey. Do visit the church, a mixture of Romanesque and Gothic, there is much to see including the sarcophagus of

Philippe I and, of course, the relics of St Benedict in the crypt. St Benôit is renowned for its Gregorian chant. Visitors are welcome.

Proceed along the D60 through lush agricultural farmland, skirting the river here and there, until you reach the old bridge leading across the river into Sully-sur-Loire.

Sully-sur-Loire

Here you can view the château (see p. 113) before continuing south to Gien.

Detour

If you stayed overnight in Sully-sur-Loire, I suggest a leisurely morning completing your exploration of the town and château before proceeding to Gien for lunch.

Leave Sully-sur-Loire by taking the un-numbered road along the riverside, which begins by passing a camp site. You have good views of the sandy banks of the Loire, and you will notice that wild flowers abound. The Nuclear Power Station is visible in the distance on the other side of the river. Turn right at the end of this little road and left when you reach the main road. Continue through St Gondon and Poilly-Lez-Gien to Gien.

Gien

There is excellent parking throughout the town, mostly on pay meters.

Lunch at Gien.

I admire Gien. It was very badly damaged in battles in 1940 and again in 1944. It has been skilfully rebuilt and they have reproduced all the original 16th-century intricate brickwork patterns which you will see throughout the town.

The château is on high ground overlooking the town and the river. The château of Gien was built by Anne de Beaujeu in 1484, she being the eldest daughter of Louis XI. The château now houses the Musée International de la Chasse, (International Hunting Museum).

I have never seen a museum quite like this, it is wonderfully laid out, and I must say I can visit it time after time and still find something new to interest me.

There are 100 paintings by François Desportes, 1661-1743, the French animal artist. There are weapons of all types used throughout history in the hunt, including the rifle of Napoleon I which he took on his shoots at Fontainbleau. There are trophies, collections of horns and various outfits and uniforms and an intriguing collection of military buttons. Throughout, there are numerous examples of the art of the taxidermist, plus beautiful animal bronzes and ceramic designs.

The museum is open daily: Palm Sunday-All Saints Day 9am-noon, 2.15pm-6.30pm and for the rest of the year it closes at 5.30pm. Tel: (38) 67 24 11.

I overheard a lovely remark on my last visit to this museum, a lady from Surrey said to her friend 'This really makes a wonderful change from looking at four poster beds.' I could not agree with her more.

From the terraces of the château you have a very good view over the Loire and the town. Before descending into the town visit the church of St Joan of Arc, which is situated in the same square. This was almost completely destroyed in 1940, but they have made an excellent job of rebuilding it. The stained glass windows are in themselves well worth a visit.

No visit to Gien would be complete without seeking out the Musée de la Faiencerie de Gien. The home of the world-famous Gien porcelain. This is situated in the Place de la Victoire, tel: (38) 67 00 05. The museum is open daily 9am-11.45am, 2pm-5.45pm. The shop which sells the porcelain made here is only open Monday to Saturday, 9am-11.30am, 2pm-5.30pm.

Leave Gien by crossing the bridge (Vieux Pont, 15th-century) and continue on the D951. As you drive along this road you will see the château de St Brisson looking down at you from a hill to your right. It was owned by one of the robber barons who was ousted by Louis VI. Just before you reach Châtillon-sur-Loire you go under the Pont Canal, which carries the Canal Lateral across the Loire to join the Briare Canal. This is an admirable engineering feat. The whole bridge is 664 metres long, it took seven years to build, 1890-97. It is the longest of its type in the world, and Eiffel (of tower fame) was a consultant on the project.

This whole stretch of river is very popular with anglers for pike, perch and the newly-introduced zander, which is very good to eat. Continue through Châtillon-sur-Loire, turn left at the sign to Sancerre and continue on the D951. Passing through Beaulieu-sur-Loire and Belleville-sur-Loire (where you will see another Nuclear Power Station on your left) continue on the D751 alongside the canal through Sury-près-Léré, and Ménétreau. Shortly afterwards, you cross the canal and carry on through Les Fouchards when the road becomes the D955. Turn right at St Satur (be careful this is a blind junction) and proceed to Sancerre.

Sancerre

As you approach the town, you will see the hills covered in a neat pattern of vineyards where the famous Sauvignon grape is grown for the world-renowned Sancerre wine. Turn left at the small traffic island at the top of the hill. You are now in my beloved Sancerre.

Sancerre means a lot to me and my family. We live here during the summer months and it is a superb centre, not only for myself where I can work and get inspiration but also for my wife, who is an artist. As this section evolves you will, I hope, understand why Sancerre is so close to my heart.

I have often heard of it being referred to as a 'Fairy Tale' village, perched as it is on top of a hill. From a vantage point called 'Le Panoramic' which is on the Esplanade Porte-César, you have an inspiring view of the surrounding countryside. You will see the river Loire at its best, winding through very picturesque woods and the vast plain that surrounds it. You are looking at this vista from an altitude of about 150m. You will see the vineyards spread out before you and in the distance La Puisaye forest and the towns of St Satur and St Thibault, which are sister towns of Sancerre.

Dinner and overnight at Sancerre

Le Rivage
1 quai Nice
Gien
Tel: (38) 67 20 53

Lovely views and good food.

Closed:	8 February—1 March
Credit cards:	AmEx, Euro, Diners, Visa
Rating:	★★★

La Loire
18 quai Lenoir
Gien
Tel: (38) 67 00 75

Closed:	September 1-15, February 3-24, Tuesday evenings and Wednesdays
Credit cards:	Visa
Rating:	★★

USEFUL INFORMATION: GIEN

Population:	17,000
Altitude:	145m
Distances:	Bourges 76km; Orléans 64km; Paris 15km
Tourist Office:	rue Anne-de-Beaujeu Tel: (38) 67 25 28

Hôtel Panoramic
Rempart des Augustins
18300 Sancerre
Tel: (48) 54 22 44

This is a modern hotel but extremely comfortable. The restaurant is good and the prices reasonable. There are wonderful views from the rear of the hotel over the vineyards.

Rooms:	57
Facilities:	Restaurant; bath, telephone, television in all rooms
Credit cards:	All major cards accepted
Rating:	★★★

Hôtel du Rempart
Rempart des Danes
Sancerre
Tel: (48) 74 55 68

This was one of Sancerre's leading establishments, but during the last few years the standard has dropped. It has just changed hands so I have high hopes that it will return to its original splendour. That is why I have included it in this book. The restaurant is very good.

Rooms:	13
Credit cards:	All major cards
Rating:	Restaurant — ★★★
	Bedrooms — ★★

Restaurant de la Tour
Place de Halle
Sancerre
Tel: (48) 54 00 81

An excellent menu, regional food a speciality. M. Fournier is the owner as well as the Chef.

Rating:	★★★★

Pizzeria
Place de Halle (under the de la Tour)
Sancerre

This is an extremely popular venue. Enormous pizzas are cooked as you watch, and are served at very reasonable prices. The varied menu includes L'Écurie, which is my favourite. This is a converted cellar, great fun, good service and an excellent wine list at reasonable prices.

If you have children, they will love this restaurant and its atmosphere. On a Friday and Saturday night it can get busy, so endeavour to get there reasonably early. It is a popular place for visiting English rugby teams.

Rating: ★★★

Auberge Alphonse Mellot
Place de Halle
Sancerre

This is situated also in the Place de Halle (incidentally the Sancerre Town Council decided to rename it Place Nouvelle, even though you may see it on maps, everybody still knows it as the Place de Halle). Joseph Mellot the Wine Producer owns this restaurant, but you can only get omelettes, goat's cheese and cheese of many varieties. Obviously plenty of good Sancerre wine. This is a lovely quiet establishment and you dine surrounded by old winemaking equipment. Try the omelette made with smoked ham, the ham is made in Sancerre and is terrific.

Wherever you choose to dine, do enjoy your meal accompanied with Sancerre Blanc, and you may be surprised to discover Sancerre Rouge and Rosé, which is seldom seen in England.

USEFUL INFORMATION: SANCERRE

Postal address:	38,000 Sancerre
Population:	2,300
Tourist Office:	Place de Halle

Château Sully

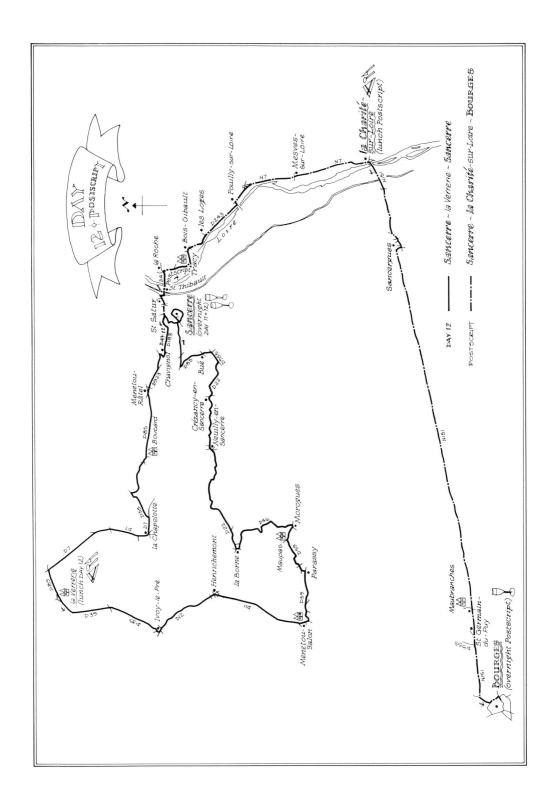

DAY 12 · POSTSCRIPT

la Charité-sur-Loire (lunch Postscript)

Mesves-sur-Loire

Pouilly-sur-Loire

Bois-Gibault

les Loges

Loire

la Roche

St Thibault

St Satur

Sancerre (overnight) DAY 11+12

Sancergues

Menetou-Râtel

Boucard

Chavignol

Bué

Crézancy-en-Sancerre

Neuilly-en-Sancerre

la Chapelotte

la Verrerie (lunch Day 12)

Ivoy-le-Pré

Henrichemont

la Borne

Moulins

Morogues

Parassy

Menetou-Salon

Maubranches

St Germain-du-Puy

BOURGES (overnight Postscript)

DAY 12

POSTSCRIPT

Sancerre ~ la Verrerie ~ Sancerre

Sancerre ~ la Charité-sur-Loire ~ BOURGES

DAY 12

Sancerre, Chavignol, La Verrerie, Henrichemont, La Borne, Sancerre: approx. 95 km (59 miles).

You will spend the morning on foot before getting back in your car once more. It will be a relaxing journey, pottering about from village to village, and leaving your car to stroll around. Lunch at the Auberge la Maison d'Hélène in La Verrerie. This is next to the château, which you may visit, or if lunch has been very good, you may prefer to sit and rest by the lake. The afternoon drive will take you through more villages of interest, including La Borne, the pottery centre and the wine village of Bué.

Overnight at Sancerre.

Map references:

Sancerre	2°50'E 47°20'N
Chavignol	2°47'E 47°21'N
Boucard	2°41'E 47°22'N
La Verrerie	2°32'E 47°26'N
Henrichemont	2°32'E 47°18'N
La Borne	2°35'E 47°17'N
Bué	2°48'E 47°18'N

Travels in the Loire Valley

Breakfast at Sancerre

Sancerre

After breakfast you could take a stroll around the narrow cobbled streets of Sancerre, but make a point of leaving the town around 11am, you will be returning at the end of the day so you can continue your walk in the cool of the evening.

Start at the Esplanade Porte-César, which offered the wonderful panoramic view on your arrival. It is just up the road from the two hotels.

Walk further up the hill and you will enter the Place de Halle (Nouvelle Place). On this square stood an old wheat market which was built in 1458 by Jean IV de Bueil, Count of Sancerre. This was pulled down and a new one built in 1883, this happened again in 1981, and now it is a lovely open space, with a fountain, and many cafés use it for their umbrella tables. One of these is the Café des Sports, this café is used by all the locals in Sancerre, making it a good place to drink a cup of coffee and watch the world go by. The French as you know love promenading, so purchase a copy of *Paris Soir* or *Nouvelle République* which is the local daily paper, pop a Gaulloise in your mouth, you will feel like one of them. On the wall of the café you will see a drawing of Azay-le-Rideau which my wife sketched for this book. Charlie and Claudine who run this establishment were presented with this, and duly had it framed, perhaps this small café will one day be called the 'Café des Arts'.

Whilst you are consuming your café noir or bière pression, let me tell you a little about the history of Sancerre. Sancerre was a very important town in the Berry region of France, and its importance was highlighted during the Hundred Years' War, fighting the English and the Burgundians. It was in Sancerre that Charles VII commandeered his army.

During the Wars of Religion in the 16th century, Sancerre became a Huguenot stronghold and gained the attention of the Royalist army who repeatedly attacked the town.

It was on the 3rd January 1573 that events came to a head. Marshal de la Chatre attacked the town and besieged it with 7,000 men. The population of Sancerre managed to keep the Royalist army at bay, and so the siege lasted for a period of seven months. During the siege the starving people resorted to eating powdered slates off the roofs of the houses and all the skins and pieces of leather they could find. After 220 days they had to surrender. In tribute to their courage, the town of Sancerre was awarded full military honours and the people allowed to practice their own religion, under the lenient rule of Henri IV.

Even today Sancerre is proud of its history, and so they should be. Fancy eating powdered slates off the roofs. As you finish your refreshment, let your eyes go around the roofs of the houses in the square and see if there are any tiles missing!

Walk to the left of the square and you will come to the Rue des Trois Pillars (Three Pillars Street). The gallows used to stand at the end of this street.

You will now see the La Tour des Fiefs (14th-century). The château was destroyed in 1621 by Henri de Bourbon, Prince of Condé. All that remains is the tower. The tower is open to the public every Sunday, from the top you will obtain a commanding view of the surrounding countryside and the newer château hidden among the trees.

You then come into the Place de la Paneterie (Breadpantry Square).

You will see the Town Hall (La Mairie) which was built in 1831. During the season an art exhibition is held here, it usually is of a very high standard. Opposite is the Clement's house (15th-century).

Walk back up the hill and you will arrive in the Place du Beffroi (the Belfry Square). The belfry was built at the beginning of the 16th century. In 1573 after the famous siege the bell and the clock were taken to Bourges as a punishment to the town. Next to the church stands a lovely 15th-century house that was owned by the grandson of Jacques Coeur, see p. 140.

Leave Sancerre by the way you entered, heading to Chavignol on the D183.

Chavignol

You can park in the main square. Across the road you will see the factory of M. Dubois, who makes Chavignol cheese, Crottins de Chèvre. Do not be put off by the name, the cheeses are sought after all over the world, and they are superb with Sancerre Blanc. Visitors are welcome at the factory and you can see the cheeses being made.

Leave the village and carry on up the road, up a very steep hill. At the top there is a splendid view of Chavignol, Sancerre and the vineyards. This hill is part of a gruelling cycle race, held every year from Paris to Bourges.

Turn left to meet D923, and carry on until you come to the village of Menetou-Râtel. This village is known for tobacco cultivation. Carry on straight through the village then take the left turning to Boucard (D85).

Boucard

On reaching Boucard turn left into the château grounds. Boucard is one of the castles on La Route Jacques Coeur, see p. 140. The château Boucard is one of my favourite small castles. The architecture comparatively simple and domestic, a mixture ranging from feudal times to the Renaissance period. Building started in 1381.

Lancelot de Boucard was responsible for its planning and it remained in his family for many years. François de Boucard who was the 5th Lord built the Renaissance wing. He was the Artillery Master to the Prince of Condé. If you walk into the entrance you will notice that he had three cannon-balls placed below each window.

Phillipe de Montault de Benac, Field Marshal of France, was banished to Boucard in the 16th century, because his wife, who was the chief lady-in-waiting at the Court, made some rather personal remarks about the lifestyle of Louis XIV. After three years he came back into favour. He started to develop Boucard, by adding farm buildings, the dovecot and the gardens but very little of the gardens remain. During the time of Napoleon, the Princess de la Tremouille lived here, and after her death the château was not occupied for about 100 years. The parents of the present owner opened it to the public. Inside you can see a good collection of 17th-century furniture and a very interesting kitchen.

The château is open daily from 10am-noon, 2pm-6pm (open to 7pm from the Saturday before Palm Sunday to September 15). During the season it is a venue for classical concerts.

Return to the main road, and continue on the D85/55/7 through La Chapelotte, past woodland, along a very straight road to the D89. A narrow and beautiful road through the forest brings you to a white fence on your left at the entrance to the château La Verrerie. Proceed down the drive and park opposite the restaurant, Auberge la Maison d'Hélène.

Lunch at La Verrerie

After lunch walk over to the château. Here you will be able to obtain a conducted tour with an English speaking guide. This lovely château is still lived in by the Count and Countess de Vogué. It was built at the end of the 15th century on the edge of a beautiful tranquil lake surrounded by mature oak trees. The château came under the influence of the Stuarts, you can see mention of them in the frescoes in the chapel. The nearby town of Aubigny-sur-Loire, was given by Charles VII to a Scotsman, John Stuart, as a reward for fighting with him against the English. After his death he was succeeded by Bernard Stuart, who reconciled Louis XI and his cousin (the future Louis XII), after years of disagreement.

He was followed by Robert Stuart who fought with François I in Italy. The presence of the Stuart family drew many of their kinsmen and followers to this part of France. Today if you look in the local telephone directory you will find many Scottish names. It is said that the leaning steeple on the Chapel was built in this way to resemble the churches on the Scottish coast which also have sloping spires facing the prevailing wind.

The Duchess of Portsmouth, whose great admirer was King Charles II of England, lived at La Verrerie from 1672 until 1734, and in 1842 one of her heirs, the Duke of Richmond — owner of Goodwood House in Sussex — sold the château to the grandfather of the present owner, the Marquis de Vogué. This château is also on La Route Jacques Coeur (see p. 140). The château is beautifully furnished and unlike many others it feels lived in. We had an informative guide who was English. The château is open from 15 February-15 November, 10am-noon, 2pm-7pm. Closed on Tuesdays.

If you ever wish to return for a longer stay, you can always book a room in the château. The rooms are simply beautiful and you certainly live in great style. It is a little expensive as you would guess, but it is worth it. You can ride, swim and fish in the lake and there are facilities for tennis. You can also have breakfast in bed, what a luxury. For details contact the Countess de Vogué, Château La Verrerie, 18700 Aubigny-sur-Nère.

After visiting the château, you can enjoy a quiet stroll around the lake before returning to your car. Drive out along the road past the lake onto the D39 to Ivoy-le-Pré, then take the D12 to Henrichemont.

Henrichemont

There is an interesting and unusual (star-shaped) square in the centre of this small town. It never fails to fascinate me. For the weekly market, it is filled to capacity, on other days it is just a vast square which seems out of proportion to the size of the town.

This is how it came about: Sully, minister to Henri IV early in the 17th century, endeavoured to build a small principality as a refuge for the Huguenots. He already had a château nearby in La Chapelle d'Angillon, but decided to build a town here in Henrichemont. In the plan there was to be a very big square with 8 roads all converging onto it, and that is what you see today. The whole scheme never came to fruition. Drive around the square with its 8 converging roads and seek out the D11 to Menetou-Salon, which is well known for its light red wine and its château. The château was built in the 13th and 14th centuries. In 1448 Jacques Coeur bought it before his collapse from public life.

Leave on the D25 (beside the church) which leads to the D59. Drive through Parassy to Château Maupas. You pass many vineyards and caves all selling the wine of Menetou-Salon. Incidentally this is extremely good and you may decide to crack a bottle at dinner tonight.

Château Maupas

You will then see the Château Maupas in the distance. Drive in the entrance which is on your left. It is compact and beautifully situated with lawns leading down to a lake. The Château Maupas was built in the 15th century by Jean Dumesnil Simon, bailiff and governor of the Berry. It was erected on a previous site which belonged to the Sullys. Antoine Agard bought it in 1682, for 36,000 F, paid in gold. He was ennobled by Louis XV in 1725. You may visit the drawing rooms, state bedroom, games room and kitchen.

Continue on to Morogues (D59) where you turn left at the church and head for La Borne (D46), along a winding country road through a valley.

La Borne

This is a little village with no more than 200 people, pretty well all of them are involved in the making of pottery, everywhere there are workshops, kilns and all things associated with the craft. Presumably the local clay has something to do with it, as there have been potters here for over 300 years. You can park at the old school which is in the centre, you cannot miss this as it is an exhibition centre, and it is well signposted.

Wandering around the village, there are plenty of opportunities to buy examples of the pottery. In the old school during the season, there is an exhibition of the work of the potters of La Borne, and upstairs during the month of August there is usually an exhibition of the work of celebrated guest potters, who are often in attendance. Almost opposite the school is a small lane, just pop down there, it will only take a minute, and you will see a most wonderful grocery shop. This looks as though it was opened at the beginning of the century and has never changed. It is not an exhibition place it is certainly for real.

Leave the village on the D22 through Neuilly-en-Sancerre and Crézancy-en-Sancerre, and take the D955 (which is the main road from Sancerre to Bourges) toward Bué.

Bué

Drive slowly through the village. Here are many of the main producers of Sancerre wine. A lovely little village, with nothing else but wine producers and vineyards (heaven!). I personally endeavour to drink Sancerre wine from Bué whenever I can.

Just in passing there is an excellent little restaurant in this village called Le Caveau, good food and reasonable prices, with an enchanting view over the rooftoops to the vineyards.

After driving through the village, go up a steep hill with vineyards on both sides. At the top of the hill, turn right at the crossroads and return to Sancerre.

Dinner and overnight at Sancerre.

Auberge la Maison d'Hélène
La Verrerie
Tel: (48) 58 31 01

This is a delightful restaurant in very lovely surroundings. The owner is Mr Jean Yvez Marec and he is assisted by a charming lady called Catherine Pernet. I put this restaurant as being one of my top restaurants on the tour. Sit back and enjoy it, it may be a good idea to reserve a table before you leave Sancerre.

The menu is fairly extensive with special emphasis on regional cooking. The chef is Jean Christophe Beaujeon who left a hotel in Paris to join M. Marec after he took over this restaurant. You will be dining in a 17th-century barn. There is an extensive wine list which has been personally selected by the owner. Should you arrive during the winter, you will find wild boar on the menu as this restaurant is frequented by people hunting in the forests.

Recommended are the Terrine de Lapin aux pruneaux, this pâté is a dish of Touraine (see p. 151); Civet de Lotte au Touraine Gamay, and Poirat du Berry, a dish from the region you are in. With your coffee ask M. Marec for a glass of Prune Liquor (15-year-old) for those who are not driving! Spend time over this meal, enjoy the surroundings and the hospitality of M. Marec.

Open all year
Prices: reasonable for this standard of
                            restaurant
Credit cards: Carte Bleu, Visa, Euro
Rating: ★★★★

POSTSCRIPT

Sancerre, La Charité-sur-Loire, Bourges: approx. 77 km (48 miles).

Today's excursion takes you to Bourges, which is the end of the tour. Leave Sancerre in the middle of the morning, and set off for La Charité-sur-Loire by a quiet and unhurried route along the riverside.

Lunch in La Charité-sur-Loire, I have recommended two contrasting restaurants to suit your mood. After visiting the places of interest, you will have a straightforward drive on a fast road to Bourges.

Overnight at Bourges, or commence your homeward journey.

Map references:
Sancerre	2°50′E 47°20′N
La Charité-sur-Loire	3°01′E 47°11′N
Bourges	2°24′E 47°05′N

Route shown p. 128.

Breakfast at Sancerre.

This is your last day of the tour. I suggest you leave Sancerre around 10.30am in time to reach La Charité-sur-Loire for lunch.

Leave Sancerre on the D955 to St Satur. Continue through the town, under the viaduct and on to St Thibault.

Just before you cross the bridge over the Loire, you could detour to the right down the quai. Here you have a wonderful view of the river and also the sandy beach which is a safe swimming area and a popular place for fishermen. Proceed across the bridge over the Loire on the D4, to La Roche. Turn sharp right on the D243 which is signposted to Tracy. In one mile take a right fork on the D553 along a shady woodland road which opens up to give a good view across a meadow on your left, of the Château Tracy. This is a private residence and is the home of one of the biggest producers of Pouilly-Fumé, the wine of the area. Continue through the village and on through vineyards. At Bois Gibault, you join the D243. Continue over the level crossing following the signs towards Pouilly-sur-Loire. At Les Loges you could park by the river, opposite the railway arch, and take a lingering look at the view over the Loire, the islands, and in the distance Sancerre. Continue between the railway line and the river until you reach the tree lined waterfront of Pouilly-sur-Loire, where the river is wide and dotted with islands.

Turn left away from the bridge and right onto the D28A, where there are plenty of caves if you wish to sample Pouilly-Fumé, and purchase a bottle or two to take home. This road leads out to the N7. You pass through Mesves-sur-Loire and on to La Charité-sur-Loire.

La Charité-sur-Loire

Follow the signs to Centre Ville and park in the Place Général de Gaulle. A large square by the Hôtel de Ville.

There is an interesting true story of how La Charité acquired its name. It was on the route to the Spanish shrine of Santiago de Compostella and the pilgrims were given a free night's lodging at the abbey, hence its name 'Charity on the Loire'.

It is a nice town for general shopping, and if you wish to take some of the finest confectionery in Berry home with you, visit the Confiserie du Prieure, at 11 Place des Pêcheurs. This is just by the entrance to the church of Notre Dame. Visit the church, which is a splendid example of Cluniac architecture. Look at the St Croix tower which was part of the 12th-century nave rebuilt in the 18th century. The choir and transepts are 11th- to 12th-century.

Lunch at La Charité-sur-Loire

Leaving Charité, you go over two bridges onto the N151. You are now on a fast straight road through agricultural land. In high summer it is bright with fields of sunflowers. The road passes through Sancergues and Maubranches. You then go over a level crossing through the town of St Germain-du-Puy leading into the outskirts of Bourges. Don't worry about all the supermarkets and Do-it-Yourself stores alongside the road. The town of Bourges had the sense to put them well outside rather than spoil the centre.

Bourges

Follow the signs to Centre Ville, then make your way up the cobbled streets of the old town, following signs to the cathedral. Here you will find good parking. If I had a choice to live in any French city, I would certainly choose Bourges (with the exception of Sancerre, but I did say city).

Bourges lies right in the centre of France, often missed by most tourists because they are all charging down the nearby autoroute to the South. It is the capital of Berry. Joan of Arc came here too. Where did she not go? I have often wondered if some towns made up the fact that she visited them, because she must have been a well-travelled young lady. She spent the winter here in 1429. During this time, she laid siege to La Charité, but abandoned the fight for lack of supplies, see p. 17.

Your first port of call is the Cathedral St Etienne. I consider this to be one of the finest cathedrals in France, certainly the finest example of Gothic architecture other than Chartres. Building began in the 12th century and continued through the 13th century. It has of course been added to since then, it has five aisles and is a massive 407 feet long with spectacular flying buttresses. Look at the stained glass windows, brilliant colours and fascinating designs, the best one to seek out is 'A meal in the house of Simon'. The relief carving over the main west door is something to be seen, if damnation is like this I will endeavour to work with something else in mind. The Duke of Berry is buried here and you can view his tomb. For a small fee you can climb the North Tower for a wonderful view, and you could take a more leisurely visit to the crypt (closed on Sundays).

The cathedral is open every day, 8am-noon, 2pm-6.30pm.

After your visit to the cathedral stroll across to the gardens beside the car park, this is very relaxing and has a renowned display of flowers and beautifully kept lawns. I wish we could have gardens like this in England, the French certainly go in for flowers in a big way, they are proud of their gardens, but alas I suppose our climate is not so suitable for growing flowers in such profusion. Bourges is known as the 'City of Flowers'. There is also the Jardin des Prés-Fichaux, which is famous for its many great topiary arches. It is considered to be one of the finest public gardens in France.

Walk past the formal pools and fountains to the Tourist Office (near the entrance to the car park), call in as there is always an exhibition taking place. Down the main street is a signpost to the Palais Jacques-Coeur.

The palace has four main buildings around a central court, it was erected in 1450 and is considered one of the finest secular Gothic buildings in France. Although none of the original furnishings remain, the wealth and detail in the decorations and a monumental chimneypiece, plus the sculptures in the great hall, show how luxurious life could be in the 15th century, if you had a fortune to spend.

Jacques Coeur also had a financial interest in sixteen of the châteaux in Berry. You can obtain booklets of La Route Jacques Coeur, with maps and details of them all. This is not the tale of romance one might have expected from his name, merely one of money and, perhaps, love of property. Jacques Coeur was a banker and finance minister who, as you can guess, became an extremely rich man, however he did not enjoy his palace for long. He overspent and became bankrupt. After a trial by jury of his debtors, he was thrown into prison by Charles VII and died there in 1456.

The Palace is one of the finest examples of 15th-century architecture. You must see the ceremonial room, the ceiling is shaped in the form of a ship's hull, and there are magnificent fireplaces.

You can have guided tours through the palace, which is open 9am-11.45am, 2pm-5.15pm during the season, in winter 10am-11.15am, 2pm-4.15pm.

Walk afterwards through the old town to see the 15th- and 16th-century half timbered houses in the Rue Bourbonnoux.

This is where I say goodbye to you, I hope you have enjoyed the tour as much as my wife and I did when researching this book. Come back again as soon as possible, you have obviously found somewhere which you want to visit again, or you have met some French friends, or like me you just truly love the area.

Dinner and overnight at Bourges.

Auberge de la Noir
La Charité-sur-Loire

Here you can obtain excellent omelettes, and on a sunny day you can sit outside and watch the house martins nesting above the entrance to the church.

Rating: ★

Grill La Sauvette
Place des Pêcheurs
La Charité-sur-Loire

The grill offers a full lunch at reasonable prices. Good menu.

Rating: ★★

Hôtel Angleterre
1 place Quatre Piliers
Bourges
Tel: (48) 24 68 51

Closed:	18 December—16 January
Rooms:	31
Credit cards:	AmEx, Visa, Diners
Rating:	★★

Le D'Artagnan
19 Place Sérancourt
Bourges
Tel: (48) 21 51 51

Open all year	
Rooms:	73
Credit cards:	Visa, AmEx.
Rating:	★★★

Recipes from
the Region

MENU 1 &

Hot Canapé of Ste Maure Cheese with Garlic

. . .

Conger Eel with Salmon and Asparagus

. . .

Strawberry Sorbet au Chinon et à la Canelle

. . .

Wine choice:
Dry white — Montlouis or Azay

Hot Canapé of Ste Maure Cheese with Garlic

1 fresh Ste Maure cheese
2 cloves garlic
12 small slices of brown bread
A handful of chives
Stock

Peel the garlic, take out the green core. Cook in white stock liquid until soft, then purée. Cut 12 slices of cheese, put them on the slices of bread. Knead the rest of the cheese with the garlic purée and the chives, chopped finely. Cover each slice of bread and cheese with this mixture and warm slowly in the oven on a low heat.

Serve on lettuce leaves.

144

Conger Eel with Salmon and Asparagus

Recipe prepared by Alain Brisacier, Chef, Hôtel Grand Monarque, Azay-le-Rideau

400g Conger eel (skinned)
300g salmon (skinned)
20g melted butter
Several fishbones — turbot, soles, brill — (crushed)
2 onions, chopped
Minced herbs: 1 clove, 2 bay leaves, 1 sprig of thyme
½ l dry white wine
¾ l water
Salt
1 kg white asparagus
4 cubes of gelatine
Juice of 2 lemons
6 sprigs of parsley
1 leek (green part)
3 shallots
Several sprigs of chervil

Serves 4

Melt the butter in a casserole dish — add the crushed fishbones, minced herbs and chopped onions. Mix well with the wine and water. Season with salt and cook at medium heat for 35 minutes. Pass the whole mixture through a sieve. In the resultant liquid poach the salmon for 8-10 minutes (according to the thickness of the fillet), and then the eel in the same way. Leave the cooked fillets to one side to cool. Reserve the poaching stock.

Meanwhile, peel and wash the asparagus, then cook until tender in slightly salted water. Tip them out onto a cloth. To make up the jelly, reduce the fish poaching stock and lemon juice to ½ litre. Add the gelatine cubes and allow to dissolve.

In a rectangular dish build up successive layers of asparagus, salmon, asparagus, eel, asparagus, in that order. Garnish with sliced shallots, flattened pieces of parsley, leek and chervil. Pour over the jelly, making sure that all the layers are covered. Refrigerate for several hours.

Strawberry Sorbet au Chinon et à la Canelle

500 g ripe strawberries
½ l red Chinon (2 or 3 years old)
250 g sugar crystals
2 tsp cinnamon

Serves 4

Cook the strawberries in the wine, sugar and cinnamon. Mix and pass through sieve. Turn out into individual dishes. Leave to refrigerate until needed.

MENU 2 &

Salmon Slices in Garlic Butter

. . .

Veal Escalopes

. . .

Clafoutis

. . .

Wine choice:
Sancerre White

Salmon Slices in Garlic Butter
(Darne de Saumon au Beurre d'Ail)

4 slices salmon
150 g butter
80 g garlic
1 carrot, diced
1 onion, sliced
½ l white wine
½ l water
Thyme
Bayleaf
Salt and pepper

Garnish
Sprigs of parsley

Serves 4

Fill a small pan with salted water and boil. Peel the cloves of garlic, and place them in the boiling water for about 10 minutes. Drain and dry the cloves, then crush the garlic into a purée (if possible in a pestle and mortar). Add the butter and pound until you get a creamy consistency. Salt to flavour.

Poach the salmon slices in a mixture of water, white wine, a little thyme, a bay leaf, pepper, carrots and onion. Simmer gently for a few minutes, remove and place on a warm dish. Top with garlic butter. Decorate with sprigs of parsley.

146

Veal Escalopes
(Escalope de Veau au Basilic)

25 g butter
4 veal escalopes
2 tsp flour
150 ml white wine
150 ml chicken stock
300 ml thin cream
Salt and pepper
3 tbsp basil leaves, cut in strips

Serves 4

First of all heat the butter in a large frying pan, and then cook the veal escalopes, turning once. Keep warm on a hot dish.

Stir the flour into the pan juices and cook for one minute, stirring all the time. Heat the stock and wine and add slowly to the pan until you get a smoothly blended texture. Then boil rapidly for two or three minutes until the liquid is reduced to about half.

Lower the heat and add the cream. Stir until completely blended, and then add salt and pepper. Allow to simmer for 2-3 minutes, before stirring in 2 tbsp basil. Pour the sauce over the escalopes in the dish. Sprinkle the remaining basil over the top and serve. This dish is wonderful with new potatoes and a fresh green vegetable, but a green salad is also a good accompaniment.

Clafoutis

675 g stoned black cherries
15 g butter

Batter
3 eggs
Pinch of salt
3 tbsp flour, sifted
A small amount castor sugar
600 ml milk, heated

Serves 4

Butter a fireproof dish which must be large enough to hold the cherries in one layer. Lay the cherries in it.

Beat the eggs with the salt, add the flour and beat again, followed by the sugar, and then the hot milk. Beat until smooth and pour over the cherries. Dot with a little butter, place in oven and bake for 30 minutes at 200°C/400°F until it is set and golden — scrumptious.

147

MENU 3 &

Aubergine Omelette

. . .

Pigeon with Foie Gras and Spring Onions

. . .

Floating Island

. . .

Wine choice:
Chinon or 10-year-old Bourgueil

Aubergine Omelette

100 g aubergine
sunflower oil
1 clove garlic, peeled
5 eggs
Salt and pepper
15 g butter

Serves 2

Peel the aubergine and cut into thin slices. Soak the slices in a bowl of salted water for about 10 minutes. Drain and squeeze dry in a cloth. Heat some sunflower oil in a frying or sauté pan, this comes up about ½ inch in the pan. Now here is the secret, when very hot, put in the clove of garlic (peeled) and the thin slices of aubergine. Cook for about four minutes, until golden brown, during this operation stir once or twice. Remove the cooked slices from the pan and drain on soft kitchen paper. Place on a hot dish and keep warm.

Beat the eggs, season with salt and pepper. Melt the butter in an omelette pan and make the omelette in the usual way. When it is almost cooked scatter the aubergine slices over the top (not the garlic clove). Fold and serve immediately. Serve with a green salad.

Optional fillings

Garlic Omelette

1 slice stale white bread
(1 cm thick)
15 g butter
1 tbsp sunflower oil
1 clove garlic (peeled)

Garnish
Chopped parsley

Serves 2

Remove the crusts from the bread and cut into cubes. Heat the butter and oil in the frying pan and put in the whole clove of garlic. When it is *very* hot, add the bread cubes, and turn frequently until golden brown. Drain the cubes on soft kitchen paper. Add to the omelette as above. Serve garnished with parsley.

Pepper Omelette

2 green, red or yellow peppers

Serves 2

Grill the peppers under a grill, turning them frequently until the skin has blackened and blistered all over. Cool them and peel off the skin (take off every little piece with a sharp knife). Cut peppers into strips, throw away the seeds and stalks. Add strips to omelette as above.

Pigeon with Foie Gras and Spring Onions

4 young pigeons (300 g each approx.) with giblets
800 g melted butter
Pepper and salt
50 g thin cream
100 g foie gras
50 ml port
30 ml champagne
150 g spring onions
40 ml meat (glaze) stock
40 ml chicken stock

Serves 4

Remove the outer coatings and poach the onions in stock enriched by a knob of butter.

Rub interior of pigeons with salt, then roast them with the giblets in the butter. After 10 minutes add the onions. Roast for a further 20 minutes, or until tender. Withdraw from heat, remove pigeons and onions and keep warm. Pour off the fat from the roasting dish and add the port. Flambé with the champagne. Let the liquid reduce then add the meat glaze. Reduce the liquid again, remove the giblets, add cream, the roasted onions and foie gras, cubed. Stir and pour over the pigeons before serving.

Serve with artichoke hearts stuffed with morello cherries.

Floating Island
Île Flottante

4 egg whites
100 g castor sugar
2-3 drops vanilla essence

Custard
300 ml milk
3 egg yolks
50 g castor sugar

Topping
100 g sugar
6 tsp water
flaked almonds

Serves 4

Rub four small basins with butter and dust with sugar. Whisk the egg whites until stiff, fold in the sugar and vanilla essence. Divide into the basins and poach in a bain marie in a moderate preheated oven for 20 minutes. Allow to cool.

Combine milk, egg yolks and castor sugar and heat gently until smooth. Divide the custard onto four dessert plates, and when cold carefully turn the 'islands' out into the middle.

Melt the sugar in the water and boil until it turns to caramel, then spin with a fork in strands across the top of the islands. Toast the flaked almonds and scatter on top.

MENU 4 &

Terrine of Rabbit with Prunes

.   .   .

Eel stew à la Touraine

.   .   .

Pear Tart

.   .   .

Wine choice:
Menetou-Salon Rouge

Terrine of Rabbit with Prunes
Recipe from M. Jean Christophe Beaujeon, Chef at the Auberge la Maison d'Hélène, La Verrerie

1 plump rabbit
250 g bacon
300 g sausage meat
20 prunes (stoned and finely chopped)
1 glass brandy
1 glass white wine (Touraine if possible)
1 tbsp olive oil
1 carrot, sliced
1 onion
1 bouquet garni

Debone rabbit and marinate overnight in wine, brandy, carrot, onion, olive oil and bouquet garni. Drain rabbit and reserve the marinade. Mince the rabbit. Add a glass of the marinaded liquid to the sausage meat and knead until a pâté is formed. Line a terrine dish with half the bacon pieces, and then build the centre in layers. First cover the base with the sausage meat pâté, next add the minced rabbit, press down firmly before adding the chopped prunes. Arrange the remaining

151

Serves 4

bacon pieces to cover the terrine and garnish with a bay leaf.

Cook in a moderate oven for 1½ hours and leave to cool for 24 hours before serving.

Eel Stew à la Touraine

1 kg eels
150 g salt beef
150 g shallots
170 g mushrooms, quartered
½ bottle white wine (Touraine preferably)
200 g butter
Salt and pepper

Serves 4

Gut the eels and cut 2 shallots into slices of about 1 cm thick. Blanche the salt beef and cut into small chunks. Fry the shallots and mushrooms in butter. Poach the eels in the wine for 30 minutes. Season with salt and pepper then add the beef chunks, shallots and mushrooms gradually. Add butter and further seasoning as necessary. Simmer until tender.

Serve with boiled potatoes.

Pear Tart

400 g puff pastry (frozen or home made)
1 kg pears
5 tbsp eau de vie (or brandy)
250 g sugar
1 egg
100 g fresh cream

Serves 4

Peel the pears, and cut into slices. Put into a dish with the eau de vie and the sugar, and let the pears macerate for 40 minutes.

Cut the pastry into two portions. Roll out one portion, and line a pastry or flan case. Drain the pear slices and place in the flan case. Reserve the juice. Roll out the remainder of the pastry to cover the flan and seal the edges with water or milk. Make a small hole in the centre. Beat the egg and brush the top of the pie with it. Cook in a hot oven for 15 minutes then reduce the heat and leave in the oven for 20 minutes.

Serve hot with the cream whipped into the juice left over from the macerated pears.

Regional Jams

Green Tomato Jam
Recipe prepared by the Hôtel Diderot, Chinon

2 kg green tomatoes
1½ kg sugar
3 lemons

Wash the tomatoes, dry and cut into thin slices. Put them into a deep dish, in alternate layers with sugar. Leave to marinate for several hours. Add the grated rind and juice of the lemons to the tomatoes, and cook gently, stirring often, for at least an hour. To test texture, pour out small drops onto a cold plate. If, when cool, the droplet wrinkles on being pushed, the jam has reached setting point. Transfer into clean, warmed jars and cover immediately.

Green Tomato Jam with Figs

1 kg green tomatoes
1 kg fresh figs
1 kg oranges
Juice of 2 lemons
2 kg sugar

Peel oranges very carefully removing as much white pith as possible, and cut into tiny pieces. Do the same with the figs and slice the tomatoes thinly. Cook the chopped fruit and lemon juice with the sugar and half a glass of water until juice sets (see above), then pour into clean, warmed jars and cover.

Gelée de Raisins

4 kg ripe, sweet grapes
4 dessert apples
½ l water
Sugar (see below for quantity)
4 tbsp kirsch

Crush the grapes and stir in the apples, diced whole, not peeled or cored. Leave to stand for two hours. Transfer to a large preserving pan, add the water and cook gently until the fruit is soft. Spread a square of muslin over a large bowl, pour in the cooked fruit, bring up the four corners and tie. Allow to drip slowly over the bowl (do not press or the jelly will cloud over).

When you have collected all the juice measure it and allow 450 g sugar to each ½ litre of liquid. Bring the juice and sugar to the boil very slowly to allow the sugar to dissolve, then boil rapidly until setting point is achieved (about 30-35 minutes). Stir in the kirsch and pour at once into clean, warmed jars. Cover immediately.

Glossary of Menu and Food Terms

MENU	MENU
Beer	Bière
Bill	Addition
Boiled	Bouilli
Bread	Pain
Breakfast	Petit déjeuner
Butter	Beurre
Casserole	Casserole
Cheese	Fromage
Chocolate	Chocolat
Drink	Boisson
Eggs	Oeufs
Fish	Poisson
Fork	Fourchette
Fried	Frite
Game	Gibier
Glass	Verre
Grilled	Grillé
Hot	Chaud
Hot course	Plat Chaud
Meat	Viande
Menu	Menu
Mustard	Moutarde
Pastry	Pâtisserie
Salt	Sel
Sandwich	Sandwich
Savouries	Bonnes bouches
Soup	Potage
Stewed	en ragoût
Supper	Souper
Sweets	Entremets
Tea	Thé
Tips	Pourboires
Toast	Toast
Vegetables	Légumes
Water	Eau

FISH	POISSONS
Anchovy	Anchois
Cod	Morue
Crab	Crabe
Crawfish	Langouste
Crayfish	Ecrevisse
Eel	Anguille
Haddock	Haddock
Halibut	Fletan
Herring	Hareng
Lobster	Homard
Mackerel	Maquereau
Oysters	Huitres
Plaice	Plie
Prawns (& shrimps)	Crevettes
Salmon	Saumon
Salmon Trout	Truite Saumonée
Smoked Salmon	Saumon fumé
Shellfish	Coquillages et Crustacés
Sole	Sole
Trout	Truite
Turbot	Turbot
Whitebait	Blanchaille

MEAT	VIANDE
Beef	Boeuf
Beefsteak	Bifteck
Calf's liver	Foie de veau
Ham	Jambon
Kidney	Rognons
Lamb	Agneau
Lamb Cutlet	Côtelette d'Agneau
Liver	Foie
Pork	Porc
Pork Chop	Côtelette de Porc au naturel
Pork Cutlet	Côtelette de Porc
Pork sausages	Saucisses
Sausages (various)	Saucissons
Veal	Veau

FOWL (including game)	VOLAILLES
Chicken	Poulet
Duck	Canard
Goose	Oie
Pheasant	Faisan
Turkey	Dindon

VEGETABLES	LEGUMES	FRUITS	FRUITS
Artichokes	Artichauts	Apple	Pomme
Asparagus	Asperges	Apricot	Abricot
Beans	Haricots Verts	Banana	Banane
Beetroot	Betterave	Currants, Black	Cassis
Brussels Sprouts	Choux de Bruxelles	Currants, Red	Groseilles Rouges
Cabbage	Choux	Figs	Figues
Carrots	Carrottes	Gooseberries	Groseilles
Celery	Céleri	Grapes	Raisins
Chives	Ciboulette	Grapefruit	Pamplemousse
Cucumber	Concombre	Lemon	Citron
Garlic	Ail	Melon	Melon
Gherkin	Cornichon	Orange	Orange
Leek	Poireau	Peach	Pêche
Lettuce	Laitue	Pear	Poire
Olives	Olives	Pineapple	Ananas
Onions	Oignons	Plums	Prunes
Peas	Petits Pois	Raisins	Raisins secs
Potatoes	Pommes de Terre	Raspberries	Framboises
Radishes	Radis	Strawberries	Fraises
Spinach	Epinards		
Tomato	Tomate		
Turnips	Navet		

Glossary of Motoring Terms

Anti-freeze	Antigel	Knife	Couteau
Axle-front	Essieu d'avant	Lubricate	Graisser
Axle-rear	Essieu arrière	Magneto	Magneto
Big end	Tête de bielle	Map	Carte routière
Bonnet	Capot	Nut	Ecrou
Boot	Coffre à baggages	Petrol tank	Réservoir d'essence
Brake	Frein	Piston	Piston
Brake cable	Cable de frein	Pliers	Pince
Breakdown	Panne	Piston ring	Ségment de piston
Carburettor	Carburateur	Pressure	Pression
Chain	Chaine	Pump-oil	Pompe à l'huile
Chassis	Chassis	Pump-petrol	Pompe à l'essence
Choke	Ajutage à l'aire	Pump-air	Pompe à l'air
Clutch	Embrayage	Puncture	Crevaison
Compression	Compression	Radiator	Radiateur
Cylinder	Cylindre	Repair shop	Atelier
Cylinder block	Bloc des cylindres	Reverse	Faire marcher en arrière
Cylinder head	Culasse	Roof	Pavillon
Differential	Differentiale	Screwdriver	Tournevis
Dipstick	Jauge de réservoir	Shock absorber	Amortisseur
Distributor	Distributeur	Spanner	Clef anglaise
Door	Portière	Spare part	Pièce de rechange
Driving mirror	Rétroviseur	Spare wheel	Roue de secours
Dynamo	Dynamo	Sparking plug	Bougie
Engine	Moteur	Speedometer	Indicateur de vitesse
Exhaust pipe	Tuyau d'échappement	Spring	Ressort
Fan	Ventilateur	Starter	Demarreur
Fan belt	Courroie de ventilateur	Steering wheel	Volant de Direction
Filter	Filtre	Switch	Interrupteur
Fire extinguisher	Extincteur d'incendie	Tappets	Culbuteurs
Fuse	Plomb	Tow rope	Corde de remorque
Gasket	Joint	Transmission	Transmission
Gearbox	Boîte de vitesse	Tyre	Pneu
Gear lever	Levier de commande	Tools	Outils
Hammer	Marteau	Water, distilled	Eau distillée
Handbrake	Frein à main	Weld	Soudure
Headlamp	Phare	Wheel, front	Roue avant
Horn	Klaxon	Wheel, rear	Roue arrière
Ignition	Allumage	Width	Largeur
Ignition key	Manette d'allumage	Window	Fenêtre
Insulating tape	Ruban isolant	Windscreen	Pare-brise
Jack	Cric	Windscreen wiper	Essuie-glace

Selected Bibliography

Terence Conran's France, with Pierrette Pompon and Maurice Croizard, 1987, Conran Octopus. (Excellent book on life in France and wonderful photographs).

The Book of France. Ed. John Ardagh, 1980, W.H. Smith & Sons.

AA Colour Guide Loire Valley, 1985, Automobile Association.

AA Discover France, 1983, Automobile Association.

The World Atlas of Wine, 1985, Michael Beazley.

The Wine Atlas of France and Traveller's Guide, Hugh Johnson and Hubrecht Duijker, 1987, Michael Beazley (essential reading for the wine lover).

The Hachette Guide to French Wines, 1985, Alfred A. Knopf. (The book I have used for reference is the American edition but this is available in France).

The Companion Guide to the Loire, Richard Wade, Collins.

The Loire, Séan Jennett, Batsford.

Guides des Hôtels-Restaurants, Logis et Auberges de France. (Published annually. Available in bookshops in England as well as France.)

Michelin Red Guide. Published annually, Pneu Michelin. (Available in most bookshops in England. This book is a must for the gourmet and the long distance traveller in France.)

Michelin road maps. (Always being brought up to date. Excellent local maps. Very useful.)

Michelin Green Guide to the Châteaux of the Loire. (English edition). (Full of information, as you would expect very well produced.)

AA/Hachette Guide to France. Automobile Association. (This is useful, and is always being brought up to date.)

The Loire Valley, 1986, Phaidon Press Ltd. (If you are interested in architecture this book will interest you.)

Châteaux of the Loire, 1978, Henry Myhill, Faber and Faber.

Many very good books on the Loire Valley were written years ago and are now out of print. A visit to a second-hand bookshop may be of help, if you browse around you can find some interesting and informative books, such as:

Holiday in the Touraine with Bon Viveur, John and Phyllis Craddock, 1956, Muller.

A Wayfarer on the Loire, E.I. Robson, 1926, Methuen.

Jean Plaidy the historical novelist has written some popular books around the châteaux, including *Medici Trilogy* and *Evergreen Gallant* (Henri of Navarre).

Index — Geographical

Index — Recipes